PHILIPPE SAMYN ARCHITECTURE AND ENGINEERING 1990-2000

MARC DUBOIS

PHILIPPE SAMYN
ARCHITECTURE AND ENGINEERING
1990-2000

Birkhäuser – Publishers for Architecture
Basel • Berlin • Boston

MARC DUBOIS

PHILIPPE SAMYN
ARCHITECTURE AND ENGINEERING
1990-2000

Main photographic work | Christine Bastin & Jacques Evrard

Translation from Dutch into English | Graham Broadribb

Layout and cover design | die ORGANISATION, Graz

Printing | Druckerei Theiss, Wolfsberg

Lithographs | Reproteam, Graz

Library of Congress Cataloging-in-Publication Data

Dubois, Marc, 1950-
Philippe Samyn: architecture and engineering 1990-2000 / Marc Dubois.--Monolingual original ed.
p. cm.
ISBN 3-7643-6067-4 (acid-free paper). -- ISBN 0-8176-6067-4 (acid-free paper)
1. Samyn, Philippe. 1948- --Criticism and interpretation.
2. Architecture, Modern--20th century--Belgium. I. Title.
NA1173.S257D84 1999
720'.92--dc21

99-26856
CIP

Die Deutsche Bibliothek - CIP-Einheitsaufnahme

Dubois, Marc:
Philippe Samyn: architecture and engineering 1990 - 2000 / Marc Dubois.
[Transl. from Dutch into English: Graham Broadribb]. - Basel ; Berlin ; Boston : Birkhäuser, 1999
ISBN 3-7643-6067-4 (Basel...)
ISBN 0-8176-6067-4 (Boston)

© 1999 Birkhäuser - Publishers for Architecture, P.O.Box 133, CH-4010 Basel, Switzerland

Printed on acid-free paper produced from chlorine-free pulp, TCF ∞

Printed in Austria

ISBN 3-7643-6067-4

ISBN 0-8176-6067-4

9 8 7 6 5 4 3 2 1

CONTENTS

INTRODUCTION

by Marc Dubois

In recent years, the work of Philippe Samyn and Partners has attracted an increasing level of international interest. One of a series of nine projects that featured in the "Monolithic Architecture" exhibition, organized in 1996 by the Heinz Architectural Center of the Carnegie Museum of Art in Pittsburgh, was the fascinating "Walloon Forestry Department Shell".[1] In that same year, Tony Robbin published a book entitled "Engineering a New Architecture" in which another project by the Samyn practice was discussed at length: the M & G Research Laboratory in Venafro, Italy.[2] It is this building in particular, which received the "Constructec Prize / European Prize for Industrial Architecture" in Hanover in 1994, that has earned the Belgian practice of Samyn and Partners a reputation in Europe's architectural scene. The Italian architectural journal L'ARCA has publicized a great number of his projects and issued two special editions covering the Samyn practice's work.[3] Foreign interest in the practice has resulted in their receiving a number of interesting invitations to take part in architectural competitions.[4] Recently commissions have also been forthcoming from the Netherlands, where Samyn built a new fire station in the municipality of Houten. In 1998 Samyn and Partners were awarded a preliminary study commission for the renovation of a large office building in Rome after prevailing over competition from Jean Nouvel and Emilio Ambasz,[5] and they are currently designing a large bridge at Copiapó in the Chilean Atacama desert.

With commissions nowadays being awarded more and more often over national boundaries, it would seem to be of little importance where the architect is from or where his practice is located. Nonetheless, the specific operating conditions vary a great deal between different countries, and this is certainly a determining factor when it comes to

M & G Research Laboratory, Venafro, 1989-1991

the framework in which architects can and must work. For example, it is more than clear that there is a major difference between, say, the Netherlands and Great Britain in the field of architectural policy adopted for managing the construction of a major building. Even within today's large borderless Europe, we can observe basic differences that define the operational framework in which it becomes possible to overstep the mere act of building and to create examples of stimulating architecture.

Belgium, a small, centrally located country, is, for many, a blank page as far as architecture is concerned. Unlike its neighbours, Belgium has had no outstanding personality who has assumed a leading role in European architecture since 1945. Anyone who leafs through architectural compendia will search in vain for names stemming from this small country, which is surrounded by France, Germany and the Netherlands. Is there an explanation for this undeniable absence? If we look at the governments of France and the Netherlands, for example, these regularly give a boost on various levels towards the improvement of the quality of architecture. Among other things, this is achieved through publications which encourage architectural competitions and the responsible choice of architects. The Belgian government, however, is noticeably indifferent. We see nothing in the way of stimuli either to make current architecture a subject of wider public debate or to strive towards the creation of notable public buildings. There is no sign of a favourable architectural climate in which the government seeks out talented architects. The absence of any significant architectural leadership from the top is amply demonstrated by the manner in which the European Community buildings in Brussels were built. If we ask who was responsible for the development of this monstrous European complex, which was, after all, the biggest building commission of the twentieth century in Belgium, little light can be shed on the matter. And as for the extension of Brussels airport in the nineties, five different architectural practices were lumped together for reasons of pure political expediency. We need not wonder, therefore, that the final result is of little architectural merit.[6] It has only been in the last five years that there has been a hint of a change in the tide, particularly as a result of the European obligation to organize competitions. Politics is gradually retreating from government contracts, while the interest of the private sector in quality architecture is growing.

Architecture in Belgium, confronted with sheer indifference, has always had to stand on its own feet within this vacuum. With a general social framework that is little interested in the construction of notable buildings, an architect must be capable of raising his own profile. In addition, he has to contend with the fact that in Belgium there is no architectural journal of international importance; rather, interesting constructions are only afforded attention in the foreign specialized press.

Belgian architects who have won international recognition since the seventies and eighties, such as Charles Vandenhove and Lucien Kroll, rarely receive commissions in their own country. They mainly receive their work from the Netherlands and France. In the nineties, a few Flemish architects have produced interesting smaller objects, mainly private commissions. Stéphane Beel and Paul Robbrecht & Hilde Daem, for example, only employ around 5-10 people. Larger practices that aim to follow a specific line in their architectural work find Belgium a very difficult environment to work in.

This is why we can truly say that Philippe Samyn has more than earned his success. With unyielding commitment

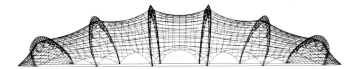

M & G Research Laboratory, structural diagram showing arches holding the roof membrane

and perhaps more than a touch of stubbornness motivating him, he has succeeded in gradually building up a multidisciplinary practice which can devote its efforts to the creation of top-quality architecture. It is quite exceptional that he has managed to achieve this within the Belgian context. The coherence of his work stands in stark contrast to the superficial results that emerge from the large Brussels practices; the latter are happy to deliver visionless plans that fit unashamedly into the soulless urban trend. Of course, Samyn knows only too well just how deplorable the state of Brussels architecture is and that his own ambition to see top-quality architecture being built in this city runs counter to the ingrained conviction that buildings are only acceptable if they are in brick and plaster. The Samyn practice has encountered considerable administrative opposition regarding a variety of project proposals in Brussels, which only goes to illustrate the difficulties.

'Samyn and Partners' has a staff of around fifty which, in Belgian terms, is a large practice. It was mainly thanks to its design for the Shell Research Centre, an impressive industrial complex at Louvain-la-Neuve (1986-1988), that the practice first attracted major attention. From here, it has succeeded in building its reputation as an extremely skilled design practice that is capable of realizing major construction projects with a considerable degree of professionalism. The list of its successful constructions is already impressive. In the Belgian architectural guide that appeared in 1996, as many as 14 of the practice's works were included.[7] Nonetheless, the true ambition of Philippe Samyn and his colleagues has long extended well beyond the borders of Belgium!

In the most significant publication to appear to date regarding Belgian architecture since 1945, Samyn himself and his position within the Belgian architectural scene are aptly described by Geert Bekaert.[8] "Nevertheless, Samyn distinguishes himself from commercial firms, to whom it does not matter whether they sell architecture or washing powder. As a typical engineer he has a strong belief in the 'universal builder', a type secretly dreamt of by all architects, who creates form out of the inventiveness of construction and discovers beauty in the laws of numbers... The most striking aspect is the continuity of his approach, in which a simple concept is chosen as a foundation to be consistently and abundantly developed down to the last detail… The structure is the form, the decoration and in some cases even furniture. Indeed, it acquires a sort of timelessness in that it is based on itself alone. This timelessness contains in it attention for the 'eternal' values of architecture – Perrault's 'absolute beauty' –, which Samyn cherishes with the greatest care, such as the quality of the materials, physical conditioning, the incidence of light, orientation, appearance, and even maintenance". Bekaert also quotes Samyn in a way that sheds light upon the aims behind the man's design approach: "I would like most of all to create an entirely traditional house. But with, for example, a façade made out of fabrics so it could be washed every week."

HIS ENGINEERING STUDIES

In order to place Samyn's work in its correct perspective, it is important to look at his training and early design career. Bekaert correctly stresses the fact that Samyn is an engineer with considerable sensitivity for a variety of construc-

Wing Building, project for a multi-function 60-storey high-rise building located in the Northern Business District, Brussels, 1972

tional aspects. His approach extends much further than a pure interest in the possibilities offered by technology. We might even say that he is a pure engineer whose approach represents a continuation of the ambition and tradition that characterized the profession in the 19th century; the devising of ingenious creations with a large dose of sensitivity for harmonious relationships. Samyn originates from a family environment in which the professional conception of creative technical solutions was the order of the day. The search for often hidden rationalism and the profound need to attain his own clarity of vision were to remain a guideline throughout the various stages on his route to becoming a significant contributor to the architectural profession.

In 1971, Philippe Samyn (*1948) received his civil engineering degree with a major distinction from the Brussels Free University (ULB), which was also his fourth year of studying architecture at ENSAAV, the architectural school of La Cambre. His thesis project at ULB concerned a multi-function 60-storey high-rise building located in the Northern Business District of Brussels. This "wing building" already clearly demonstrates Samyn's drive, his search for the expressive power of the structure and his ambition to conceive creative and attractive constructions. Furthermore, his search for a considerable degree of flexibility is already apparent in this design.

It was thanks to a scholarship that Samyn had the opportunity to continue his studies at the famous Massachusetts Institute of Technology (MIT) in 1972, where he gained the title "Master of Science in Civil Engineering". These studies covered the numerical calculation of structures. Following his return to Belgium, he not only worked as a consulting engineer but also continued his theoretical research including his analysis, entitled "Isobarres & Isonodes: Structural morphological studies on reticulated systems" which he completed in 1975. In 1974 he was granted a patent for double curvative shells with corrugated steel sheets. In 1973 he was awarded the title of urban planner from Brussels University (ULB).

What is striking is that Samyn did not choose a purely academic, theoretical career even though he could have done so. Instead, he preferred to apply himself to the real world of designing buildings, giving himself the opportunity to put his theoretical and technical insights to practical use. He first worked together with the architect Albert De Doncker in order to learn the tools of his trade. Then he opened his own practice in 1977 which he gradually expanded to form the multi-disciplinary team of Samyn and Partners. Here, he paid major attention to an optimal organization of his practice as well as its professional management. It is quite clear that it isn't just through the application of state-of-the-art software that interesting buildings have been conceived. The structure of the practice has been conceived so that a rigorous intellectual effort is applied to every project to which everyone in the team can contribute. Quality control for Samyn and his colleagues extends further than the ISO 9001 standard. It is an attitude that is not just concerned with producing good buildings. Rather, the aim is to conceive and achieve an architecture that merits the adjective "notable".

Samyn did not follow a "classical" architectural training. It was not until 1985 that he obtained his degree in a government examination. It is obvious that his approach is essentially based on engineering. But this does not mean he has neglected other important aspects. His work is infused with a consciousness that a building also holds urban-planning, physiological, ecological and cognitive dimensions. In interviews and lectures, he is capable of placing the

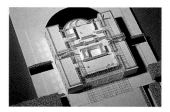

Auditorium, Brussels Free University, Anderlecht, 1992-1993   CNP-NPM Head Office, Gerpinnes, 1995-1997

various aspects of architecture within a broader historical context. He assumes clear standpoints with regard to the meaning of architecture and the role of the designer, points of departure that are consistently expressed in the subsequent design. He does not seek to avoid the difficult question of the current position of architecture or the place of the designer within the ever more complex building process.

Anyone who examines his entire oeuvre will inevitably be struck by its strict geometry. The symmetry of his architectural compositions is a prominent feature. In an interview with Pierre Loze, Samyn refers to the writings of the Dutch monk and architect Dom van der Laan, especially in his book "Architectonic Space".[9] It is not so much Van der Laan's use of brick that he is interested in, but rather his search for the meaning of relationships in architecture. Geometry remains fundamental at all times for Samyn and he believes that the way in which relationships are applied demand the architect's unmitigated attention. He remarks that the golden section, the most common system applied since the Renaissance, is no more than a method of applying two-dimensional proportions. Samyn prefers the use of Pythagoras's triangle (3,4,5) which permits the arrangement of a three-dimensional composition. In designing the CNP-NPM office building at Gerpinnes, a project that will be discussed in detail later in this book, he makes use of the triangle to apply the dimensions to space. However, there is no need to explain this using diagrams, since relationships are part of the building's very spirit. Central to the CNP-NPM building as well as other Samyn constructions is the question of the meaning of 'classical', and of the relationship between a classical aspiration and a high-tech approach. In the case of other European architects too, these are questions that constitute an essential aspect of their work: Sir Norman Foster and to a certain extent, Dominique Perrault, for example.

"I believe more than ever that the traditional and the modern as well as the traditional and the inventive, can go hand in hand," asserts Samyn, though he goes on to add that the obsessive search for the new is no more than a dreadful illusion, as though it were always necessary to invent something new. He also puts in a plea for the application of inventiveness in more fundamental areas, such as the design of more energy-efficient buildings in terms of their basic concept, rather than a mere tinkering with the insulation materials. His plea for the creation of buildings with a double glazed shell also derives from the idea of handling a commission in a conceptual manner. The question of the significance of technology then moves into sharp focus.

A characteristic feature of Samyn's work is his preference for restrained and lucid compositions, whereby he favours simple geometric volumes. His ultimate goal is to attain a "calm simplicity" in architecture, in which the need to articulate the construction and particularly the facilities disappears. It is a matter of conceptualizing intelligent technical buildings in which the dominant image of technology is severely diminished in a decisive act by the designer to attain a level architectural playing field. This is not a plea for impoverishment or comfortable emptiness. Rather, it demands considerable commitment and technical insight to achieve such restraint. The major Aula Magna project at Louvain-la-Neuve is significant in terms of this consistent development within Samyn's work and his opposition to the sensationalism of a building.

It would be incorrect to label Samyn's work as "high-tech". In summing up the characteristics of productivism, Kenneth Frampton accords significance to flexibility and the pronounced treatment of the technical facilities.[10]

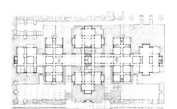

Royal Secondary School, Waterloo,
1977-1984, ground floor plan

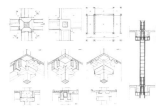

Royal Secondary School, Waterloo,
1977-1984, details of the construction

Design Board / Behaeghel & Partners, office
and studio for graphical computers, Waterloo, 1986-1988

In Samyn's work, flexibility is indeed a constant matter for consideration, but the explicit treatment of the technical infrastructure is avoided. Instead, for constructions like bridges, it is their expressivity that is emphasized, not due to a formal requirement but deriving from the constructional logic.

Samyn remains faithful to Cartesian geometry. Not for him, those complex spaces with continuous curving surfaces that today's software programs can conjure up. His work stands diametrically opposed to the approach that aims to liberate architecture from its constructional straitjacket through the use of virtual architectural images. The pressure to capture and recount the dynamism and speed of our changing society in "showy images in stone", which only make use of curved lines and surfaces, is regarded as an architectural approach that is too formal. We might well ask whether architecture can hope to supply an answer to today's compulsive search for "new things". Inventiveness must be channelled into serving more fundamental aims. Samyn considers it desirable that "building becomes more of a craft, less fleeting, less ephemeral".[11] However, this is anything but a plea for a return to the artisan-based building tradition of former epochs; rather, it seeks to place the emphasis on a more concrete requirement and a combinational approach.

For Samyn, architecture is in need of a more modest attitude, though this does not mean it should take a neutral stance. Buildings need to supply the framework in which life's activity can unfold. As the frontier between architecture and construction fades, the path of a formal dynamism that is subsequently worked out in terms of the construction is no longer the path chosen. The computer is capable of producing seductive virtual images that aim to completely divorce themselves from the internal logic of the materials. Samyn is deeply opposed to these seductive computer representations and abstract models that have little to do with the materials employed.

As well as using sophisticated computer programs in its work, the Samyn practice makes very intensive use of the possibilities offered by modelling.[12] Scale models are very often produced just to win over the client. This is a three-dimensional means of representation that has been used since the times of the Renaissance. It permits a visualization of the project alongside the drawings, as well as giving the designer the opportunity to make improvements. If, for example, we compare the model of the Brussimmo building with the final outcome, we can safely say that the latter represents an improvement. A study model, which is made for all projects, is followed by extremely true-to-life models that go as far as possible in portraying the reality of the actual building.[13] This is a very work-intensive representational method. However, it is also used due to Samyn's sheer fascination with the stimulating tradition of the engineer's model. Before the computer age, the model was an indispensable tool for the engineer in his investigation of structural possibilities. Samyn's first model, for the 1971 Wing building, was created for this reason. Even though the possibilities offered by computer simulations are constantly on the increase, the production of a model remains an essential tool in the design process at the Samyn practice. The intense interaction between the computer image and the model enhances the various stages of the design process en route to the final version. Furthermore, Samyn views the large collection of scale models that the office has produced over the years as the practice's "memory". Placed together in one large space, the models offer future clients and new work colleagues the opportunity to get to know the practice's work and history in an intensely visual fashion. The past is not simply

Shell Chemical Research Centre, Louvain-la-Neuve, extension phase 2 & 3, 1986-1988, 1990-1991

erased; what has been designed retains its place within the practice, offering the opportunity for objective reflection that can boost the intensity of future commissions.

CAREER BEGINNINGS

It is frequently true, and this is particularly the case in Belgium, that architects get their first opportunity to prove themselves in the private residential sector. The detached Boulanger residence in Ohain (1976-1979) represents Samyn's first built work that attracted public interest. His preference for a strict symmetrical layout, both of the floor plan and the volume itself, is the guiding principle here. The stepped layout of the building follows the contours of the site whereby an interesting internal configuration evolves.

Samyn's first major public commission was the Royal Secondary School of Waterloo (1977-1984), carried out in association with the architect De Doncker. The floor plan has an entirely symmetrical layout consisting of five sections of differing heights. This allowed the 18,000 m² building to be better integrated into its surroundings. However, most attention was paid to the development of an especially creative prefabricated concrete skeleton whose bare, exposed version and whose finished version are one and the same. The shape of the beams permitted easy placement of the vertical walls, while the use of a strict lattice renders the interior highly flexible. Exposed brickwork was incorporated into the façades as infill for the concrete skeleton frame.

At the beginning of the eighties, Samyn was commissioned to build private residences and apartment buildings as well as to convert interiors. In a school building in Athus (1981-1984), he made use of octagons in the floor plan. Although this work was created with enthusiasm and a great deal of care for detail, these early objects are characterized by a certain stiffness. We can clearly see that this was a period of "trial and error", with bricks and concrete being the principal materials used. Seen retrospectively, this was a significant learning phase for Samyn from which he crystallized his vision to move in certain set directions. Objects with a powerful structural division, such as the Farr residence (1984-1986), show us that Samyn was in search of a distillation of the building's expressive power deriving from the logic of the construction. This is likewise true in the case of an unbuilt design for prefabricated school buildings in Morocco (1982). Samyn's most exciting projects are those in which he uses wood for the structure, as in the aforementioned Farr residence and in the offices for the Design Board, Behaeghel & Partners (1986-1988). Given that the site for this small office building lies within a residential zone, the design was accorded a restrained, oblong form. The way in which a timber skeleton was used here was later improved upon and used in another small office building commissioned by Eric Boulanger in Waterloo (1988-1990). The surprising aspect of this is the introduction of a circular floor plan and the recessed layout of the roof. From a distance, one is reminded of a Chinese garden pavilion. Renaat Braem and André Jacqmain had already used the idea of creating a round office building in green surroundings for their stunning Glaverbel realization in Brussels (1963). Even though the shell and materials of

   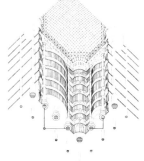

Solvay / Central Laboratory,

extension of the laboratory, Neder-Over-Heembeek, 1988, model and typical floor

Building "Au Bon Marché" / transformation, mixed-use

containing office and retail space, Brussels, 1987-1988, model and drawing of the atrium

the two buildings are entirely different, Samyn also chose a circular volume in order to optimize the garden planting. Whereas in his wooden constructions of the eighties, the emphasis was on the layout, his nineties' experimentation is mainly geared towards lightness of the construction, with the timber dome at Marche-en-Famenne being the main feature of this period.

AN INITIAL TURNING POINT
Shell Research Centre | Louvain-la-Neuve (1986-1988)

At the end of the sixties, the Belgian government decided to split the ancient University of Louvain into two universities, one Dutch-speaking and the other, French-speaking. As part of the overall plan to transfer the French-speaking university, the new town of Louvain-la-Neuve was created, the first and only new Belgian town to be founded in the course of the twentieth century. Considerable effort was put into attracting companies involved in research to move to this new site. For its new research department, Shell was allocated a site in an interesting landscape. In developing the basic concept, both the various elements of the design agenda and the layout of the site were taken into consideration. The fan-like setting that resulted was to allow for potential future expansion at the ends of the two wings.

The division of the volume, the massive brick walls and above all, the curved openings in the façades bring directly to mind associations with the work and ideas of the architect Louis I. Kahn. The Shell building exhibits a pronounced desire to assume a monumental appearance; mass and form are used in order to boost the building's expressive power. The emphatic solidity of the wall provides a link with the station and the adjoining university halls of Louvain-la-Neuve, designed in 1976 by Yves Lepère.[14] Here we see an industrial complex of considerable architectural merit, an outcome rarely attained in commissions of this sort in Belgium. One undisputed major achievement is the fact that less than two years elapsed between the initial discussions with the client and the entering into service of this 25,000 m² complex. Equally exciting is the fact that this building represents a turning point in Samyn's career. His use of brick gradually disappears to almost nothing as he moves on to a major preoccupation with the particular question of optimizing steel constructions with glass façades.

It need therefore come as no surprise that with the Shell complex as his reference work, Samyn was rapidly awarded a series of major commissions for research centres. In 1988 he was asked to restructure and provide an additional 30,000 m² to the Petrofina chemical research centre at Feluy. This was a commission that was mainly concerned with considering how the existing buildings might be reorganized as part of an overall restructure. The most significant part of the commission was the creation of a new means of access to the site which resulted in the construction of a new, private bridge across the Brussels-Charleroi canal. The bridge is especially elegant due to the slender nature of its construction. Its deck has a wooden finish that allows it to integrate better into the surrounding land-

Bank Brussel-Lambert (BBL)
"Marnix" project, preliminary
design proposal, Brussels, 1987, model

Auditorium Caterpillar,
200-seat auditorium Gosselies, 1988, model

Fina Service Station, Aire d'Orival, Nivelles, 1998-2000, model and computer image

scape. This bridge reveals the designer's true colours; here is a man who is passionate about designing attractive civil technology projects. In the eighties and nineties, the Samyn practice received major commissions for laboratories from chemical and pharmaceutical companies such as Solvay, Merck Sharp & Dohme and SmithKline Beecham. In 1988 two different designs were developed for the extension of Solvay's central laboratory at Neder-Over-Heembeek. The first proposal was for an oblong volume equal in length to the existing building. The façades were to be constructed using the double skin principle. The second proposal was based on a compact triangular ground plan in which major attention was paid to the options for filling in the atrium with circular meeting rooms. The triangular form of the exterior was further enhanced by placing the stairwells and the sanitary facilities in the corners. At the same time, while working on the Shell complex, the Samyn practice developed two major urban projects which were not to be realized. The "Au Bon Marché" project in the centre of Brussels involved the transformation of a former giant warehouse from the thirties into an office building. Here, the emphasis was placed on the reopening of the large central atrium so as to introduce sufficient daylight back into the heart of the building. More significant in terms of his office-related research is Samyn's proposal for the extension to the Bank Brussel-Lambert, which is close to the Royal Palace in Brussels. In 1987 the bank asked a series of architects to consider how this stunning building, built in 1959-1960 and designed by the American architect Gordon Bunshaft of the S.O.M. office, might be extended. Samyn's proposal foresaw a lower volume on the three sides facing the street, while in the middle, a tower of eleven storeys was planned in combination with a sloping glazed patio. In the end, the directors awarded the contract to S.O.M. (with Samyn) who repeated the existing volume.

THE SEPARATION OF THE ROOF AND THE INTERIOR

The idea of developing the roof as a completely independent object under which a whole series of activities can take place makes a regular appearance in the annals of twentieth century architecture. In one of Le Corbusier's last works, "Maison de l'Homme" in Zurich, this is the main theme. For Samyn, the separation of the roof from the building's interior has been one of his recurring themes in the nineties. The concept of developing an extremely lightweight shelter under which different volumes could be freely placed can be seen for the first time in Samyn's design for an auditorium for the firm Caterpillar in Gosselies (1988). Given the close proximity of an airfield, the acoustic requirements for the building were very high. The outside shell consists of a metal structure which is strengthened and supported by pairs of three-dimensional portals, whose arched trajectory is actually a sort of spatial projection of the flexion patterns of an "ideal" portico. The auditorium seating 200 people is an independent volume, with the stairwells integrated into the side walls. The independence of both the projecting room and the volume containing the sanitary facilities is also stressed. The auditorium's roof is a network of cables in the form of a hyperbolic parabola, covered in a transparent PVC membrane. The shelter acquires an elegant appearance thanks to the gently sloping roof and the two inclined outer walls. The auditorium has been designed as a wooden box which puts even greater emphasis on the tension that exists been the roof and the interior. Samyn's considerable affinity with wood as a material is also present in this design. The concept behind the project, which was never realized, formed the

Fina Service Station,
Aire d'Orival, Nivelles, 1998-2000

Fina Service Station, Aire de Froyennes, Tournai, 1998-

basis for a number of projects carried out in the nineties, including the fire station in Houten (1998-1999). Here, the basic volume is a large shelter, a large metal "shed" in the form of a parabola.

HIS FIRST FOREIGN COMMISSION

It was clear that Samyn, in his fascination for especially lightweight constructions, would come to direct his attention towards the potential offered by membrane constructions. In addition to the major influence of Frei Otto's work, it was the Haj Terminal Airport in Jeddah (1981), by Skidmore, Owings and Merrill, developed in conjunction with the well-known engineers Horst Berger and David Geiger, that particularly excited Samyn's imagination.[15] A commission awarded in Venafro, Italy (1989-1991), located near Naples, gave him a unique opportunity to use a membrane construction. The construction time, from digging the foundations to the entering into service of the building, was a mere eight months: a tight requirement. The building commissioned was a new research centre for plastics that is capable of withstanding a severe earthquake. Samyn used an enclosing envelope under which he placed the volumes. The structure includes six curved space framework girders beneath which a double curved polyester shell is attached. The shape of the girders is based on the most efficient solution for attaching the membrane. And once again, this commission demonstrates that a building's expressive power can be boosted without forsaking the constructional element. The rotation of the framework to locate the tip uppermost occurred for visual reasons. In terms of the potential for this type of construction, Tony Robbin stresses that "the Venafro project is important in the history of membrane structures because of its use by a private company; it is not a stadium or any other public building. Samyn's structure shows that soon perhaps membranes will have expanded applications".[16] Robbin also rightly observes that "the Venafro structure is successful because the membrane constitutes the whole building; it is not just a roof tacked onto a conventional building". As well as the technical aspect of the conception, we should note a series of important visual elements. It is no coincidence that, in publications dealing with membrane applications, these have often been photographed at night. This is because, in the darkness, the building is transformed into a giant magical beacon, with the envelope assuming a totally different significance. This Samyn construction was awarded the German Constructec Prize in 1994 and has been presented in many publications on membrane applications.[17]

ALONGSIDE THE MOTORWAYS

The major recognition Samyn received for the project in Venafro encouraged him to continue his investigations into potential membrane applications. When the oil company Petrofina decided to adopt a fresh architectural approach for their "Fina" service stations on the occasion of their 75th anniversary, they approached Samyn to help in devel-

OCAS Steel Applications Research Centre,
Zelzate (Ghent), 1989-1991, model

Euroclear Operation Centre,
competition project, Brussels,
1988, drawing

Building Bernheim-Outremer,
Office and apartment building, Brussels, model and realization, 1992-1998

oping a new corporate identity. The Fina Service Stations in Wanlin (1994-1995), located alongside the Brussels-Luxembourg motorway, were the first result of this collaboration. Anyone who searches our European motorway network for interesting constructions will soon notice that it is very rare indeed that an oil company applies any imagination to their service stations. The standard contract usually calls on work by graphic artists and style specialists, with the architectural aspect being of secondary importance. It was not until the nineties that oil companies started investing in good architecture by consulting top architects, as for example Spain's Repsol who retained Norman Foster. Fina, in retaining Samyn, have set an example for others to follow, something we should not underestimate in the development of these sort of infrastructure projects. The departure point for the Fina service station in Wanlin is the concept of the roof as a large umbrella. Back in 1989, Samyn was already using the idea of an umbrella in a project for a water tower in Mauritania. Almost all the canopies above petrol pumps have a flat, rectangular roof, a shape which is nearly impossible to integrate into any landscape. In the wooded Ardennes mountains, the shape of the membrane roof fits better into the hilly landscape. An arched-truss-supported membrane was chosen. Through this construction method alone, the project broke with the traditional solution of the flat canopy.

Service stations with associated infrastructure rarely exhibit any architectural qualities and are frequently windy locations. Under commission from Fina Europe and in conjunction with the Von Karman Institute, a new concept was developed with the aim of improving the microclimate around the petrol pumps. The point of departure for the architectural concept was the creation of a more pleasant environment. The first project in this new generation of Fina service stations is due for completion in 1999 in the Dutch municipality of Houten. To begin with, the concept of the canopy is different. It has become a sloping roof supported by elegant columns. Large transparent cylindrical sheets in expanded galvanized steel have been positioned around the service station in order to diminish the wind turbulence dramatically.

Constructions that span motorways for the accommodation of restaurants are mostly ungainly and exhibit little architectural merit. In 1998, the Samyn practice won a competition for a commission of this type near Nivelles, located south of Brussels. Both the restaurant and the infrastructure for the two service stations have been linked to form one elegant gesture. In order to obtain a flowing line, the traditional girder has been substituted by two trusses of the Warren type with a length of 210 metres. There are two support points that are positioned 70 metres apart. The petrol pumps are located beneath the large roof. Escalators placed in glass tubes transport the public up to the restaurant. In his explanatory notes, Samyn points out that motorway rest stops have been neglected for far too long and have only been designed from a very blinkered commercial perspective. He asks the pertinent question of why these locations have not been given a cultural dimension.

The commissions from Fina have given Samyn the opportunity to continue his research. The arrival of new materials such as three-dimensional textiles has led to the development of new projects based on a totally different approach and to the concept of buildings more like scarabs or shellfish where the structure is totally external and protective. The idea is to conceive the roof and wall structure as one single big bird's cage, taking advantage of the extraordinary strength and stiffness of reticulated shells. The totally exposed and permeable structure supports and

Convention Hall Nara, Japan, international competition entry, 1991

Restoration and transformation of the 18th-century "Stassart" farmhouse into architectural studios for Samyn and Partners, Brussels, 1992-1993

protects the soft internal skin and flesh, which in turn protects the equipment, the services and the restaurant. The first project of the "scarab" generation was designed for a service station on the A8 Brussels – Lille motorway near to Tournai (Aire de Froyennes). Here, not just the organic form of the roof presents us with a new approach, but also the manner in which the structure is combined with a continuous green verge. As well as improving the level of comfort, this complex is also better integrated into the landscape. A motel with a circular floor plan and a green patio is also included.

INTEGRATION OF LANDSCAPE AND CITYSCAPE

The integration of a strong architectural image with a landscaped approach is already evident in Samyn's Shell complex at Louvain-la-Neuve (1986-1988) and his OCAS research centre[18] at Zelzate (1989-1991). In the OCAS project, an oblong beam was positioned between two parabolic research halls. By encircling the building with water, an emphasis has been placed on the access routes, while the building appears rooted to its island thanks to the inclusion of green banks. In 1993, this industrial complex won the European Steel Design Award. The landscape has also played an important role in more recent designs by Samyn, such as in his design of the industrial site at Le Crachet (1995) and the extension for Seghers Engineering (1997). The "genius loci", or site potential, has been achieved through the design.

In urban designs too, the relationship with the specific features of the site has been definitive. Samyn rejects an integration that is based upon a near-obligatory urban reconstruction, a return to that style of building in which the façade was the expression of a stony architecture. His proposal for a circular office tower on the corner of the major Leopold II boulevard and the Noordwijk in Brussels is illustrative of an approach that takes into account the town-planning potential of the site. In this unbuilt Euroclear Operation Centre (1988), the building is split into four different elements so as to both boost its expressive power and to mark the corner site. A double glass skin was chosen so as to make the tower as transparent as possible. The care Samyn takes in placing the building in exactly the right position is also evident in his competition entry for the Kredietbank (1990) as well as in his design for the unrestrained Westbury Tower (1998), both located in Brussels.

The office building for Bernheim-Outremer (1992-1998), located in the Brussels Cinquantenaire-Jubilee Park, has a very specific roof shape. The double curved roof surface solved the problem of corner edges and the difficult connection with a much smaller volume in an adjacent side street. The fact that this elegant solution took years to be approved says a lot more about the buildings administration in Brussels than about Samyn's work. In the construction of the façade of this office building, Samyn has striven to include elements that will facilitate the reflection of daylight into the interior. This attention to detail derives from an energy-conscious attitude that is far removed from any mere formal preoccupation. The idea of a building based on a circular plan forms a recurring idea in Samyn's work. The continuous façade of a cylindrical building emphasizes its independent character since there is no definite

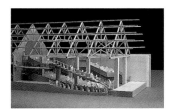  

Transformation of the Bedoret farm of the historical abbey of Gembloux, 550-seat auditorium, agronomic faculty Gembloux, 1994-1996

Scientific and technical forum "Le Crachet", Frameries, limited design competition, 1995-1997, model

direction it can underscore. An illustration of the town-planning dimension Samyn applies to his work is to be seen in the large auditorium for the Brussels Free University (1992-1993). The completely glazed cylindrical volume, housing a circular hall, strongly emphasizes the building's central significance within the campus. Nevertheless, the campus possesses a diversity of building styles that remain undiminished by the new auditorium project. The choice of a continuous façade to better underline a building's urban presence likewise occurs in Samyn's competition entry for the Convention Hall in the Japanese town of Nara (1991). A perforated aluminium shell is incorporated around an oval ground plan. Underneath the shell is the building itself as well as outdoor rooms.

BUILDINGS WITH A DOUBLE SKIN

In his research into environmentally friendly buildings that have modest energy consumption, Samyn advocates the use of the double skin concept. He has refined this concept in various projects he has developed since 1986, like his proposal for BBL and Solvay I & II. The first example of the concept that was actually built is the Brussimmo building in Brussels (1989-1993). Not only is this the first ever Belgian building using the double shell concept, but it is also a pioneering achievement within Europe. The concept of the façade also offers a solution against the high level of noise pollution to which the site is subjected. The doubling of the façade offers a whole series of advantages that are further developed in various designs by the practice. In his concept for the Aula Magna at Louvain-la-Neuve

(1996-2000), now under construction, this particular departure point forms the essence of the entire design. This is the most advanced design concerning flexible use of space, acoustic conditions, daylighting and low energy consumption. With its exposed concrete structure offering a proper thermal mass and its generalized double skin around the closed and open foyer zones as well as the highly insulated main auditorium, this building will require only a very low heat input in wintertime and practically no mechanical cooling during the rest of the year. In addition to these technical aspects, this new auditorium also makes a powerful town-planning statement in the heart of Louvain-la-Neuve.

The Dupuis office building at Marcinelle (1993-1995) is the most accomplished realization of the double skin concept to date. It also has a revolutionary plan for an office building; no single office space even touches the outer façade. This is a building in which the three atria form component units of the double skin. Air is distributed in the offices through variable air volume units and expelled through the atrium, directly to the outside in summertime, and through a heat exchanger in wintertime. The building also illustrates the major potential to be uncovered through the more imaginative use of materials. His use of crystal clear glass gives the building a greater level of transparency. In the Dupuis building, the inner walls are in glass and wood, whereas metal is used for the façade. This lends the interior a unique character. The double skin has become crucial for many other designs by Samyn. For the auditorium at the Brussels Free University, glass is used in a continuous glazed curtain around the closed volume of the big hall. The zone between the glass and the hall wall functions, together with the foyer, as the double skin. In his proposal

  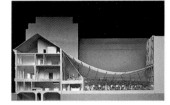 

"Groenhof", transformation of a 19th-century building, Flanders, 1997-1999   Reception lounges and restaurant for Petrofina, Brussels, 1994-1995, model and interior

for the INP building in Santiago, Chile (1997), the double skin is used as a vertical insulation zone in order to obtain natural ventilation. However, Samyn does not just propose the use of a double skin in new buildings, but includes the idea in renovation proposals too, as for example in the mining complex at Le Crachet.

RENOVATING OLD BUILDINGS

At first sight, one might imagine that working on existing buildings was of secondary interest to Samyn and that this area could only be expected to yield second-rate results. However, this is not at all the case since Samyn displays an identical attitude towards renovation projects and new buildings. There is no need to go into detailed explanations of the technical solutions to demonstrate that an architect has worked on these projects. And there really is no need for any clash between the new and the old. The designer merely has to reach decisions that render the existing real estate suitable for its new purpose, whereby the formal aspects are just a partial concern. The radical confrontation of old versus new is not a valid departure point for Samyn. In 1993 Samyn & Partners moved to offices located on the outskirts of the Zoniënwoud. This site was an agricultural complex offering the opportunity of conversion to a new use. The "Stassart" farm, the heart of which was built in 1830, was converted and extended and offers a good example of Samyn's method of treating heritage sites. The existing L-shaped volume, itself imposing, was extended by another, low L-shaped volume with a slight roof pitch and continuous large windows. This allowed the creation of a new outdoor courtyard. A large water feature imparts a tranquil character to the interior space, akin to a monastic retreat. This conversion has avoided any spectacular alteration to the existing building; the creation of a tranquil working atmosphere and the provision of a generous amount of working space (measuring around 2,600 m²) for the team were the chief priorities. The approach adopted in this conversion was not an aesthetic one; instead, the primary aim was to refer back to the basic topology of the entirely surrounded inner space encountered in old farmhouses and monasteries. In fact, the emphasis was very much placed on the existing complex. The red brick façades were restored and all traces of the conversion were left visible.

This same consistent attitude of Samyn's is also apparent in other projects. The agricultural faculty in Gembloux is housed in an imposing historical complex comprising a former abbey with ancillary agricultural buildings. Samyn was commissioned to convert the gigantic barn of the Bedoret farm of 1762 – a listed building – into an auditorium seating around 550 people. Of the twelve bays, six were used in the auditorium, which was conceived in such a way as to leave the existing spatial structure virtually untouched. Two stilts were removed and the side balconies attached to the roof structure in order to maximize visibility onto the podium. The technical infrastructure was integrated so that it is hardly noticeable, while the potency of the existing structure was further emphasized. Through this project, Samyn was able to demonstrate that a fascination with technical solutions need not result in obtrusive alterations. In 1994 his practice won the competition to renovate and extend the Brussels Brugmann hospital. Samyn succeeded in treating this commission in an intelligent way that was sympathetic with the style of its famous Belgian architect, Victor Horta. This building is one that has not been fully recognized in terms of its architectural merit.

   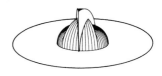

Wood museum / Hobo, Dranouter, 1991, model and drawings

Samyn's restoration proposal for the Orangery at the castle of Seneffe (1995), to be completed in the summer of 1999, was also entirely correct in its treatment of Belgium's architectural heritage.

His biggest renovation project is the ambitious competition entry for the Le Crachet mining site at Frameries (1995). As part of an investment programme by the Walloon government, an abandoned industrial site was transformed into a forward-looking scientific and technical theme park. One of its most significant features is the inclusion of a glazed protective mantle around both the buildings and the imposing mineshaft. Using his experience with double skin constructions, he used the tower both as part of the natural ventilation system and as a simultaneous protection of the metal structure. The design is equally exciting in terms of its landscaping. The existing hill on the site was reshaped to form a cone. A spiral-shaped footpath to the top was incorporated, where a panoramic viewing point was combined with a water reservoir and a windmill. The axis between the hill and the covered mineshaft apportions the outdoor space. It is noteworthy that ultimately the client chose the exciting proposal designed by Jean Nouvel which in actual fact does not represent a rejection of Samyn and still permits the latter's design to be realized. The owner of Seghers Engineering had the idea of using an old industrial complex as the framework for a high technology company. The old "Lamot" brewery, situated alongside the river Rupel at Willebroek, was converted into an office building with minimal alterations. Samyn has been very restrained in this project, as in the commissions mentioned above. The new annexes were camouflaged, but were added with a careful eye for detail so that the essence of the original building remained undisturbed. In 1997, this complex was nominated in the competition for the year's best new Belgian office building.[19]

Samyn also converted a country castle for the same client. This was built in the 19th century, but in this case was not on the official heritage protection list. "Het Groenhof" in Malderen was left intact, with the window apertures remaining untouched. The most significant addition was the placing of a large free-standing glass wall against the front façade and the inclusion of a system of solar panels behind it. This transparent screen creates a rustic atmosphere that functions as a guiding element in the design of the garden. For Samyn, this external wall represents far more than the mere inclusion of a technological infrastructure. At the same time it is a restrained sculpture that reflects the light in a flux of constant change. Here, light is both an energy form and a significant architectural element. In conversion commissions, Samyn has sought to respond to the needs of the client by intervening decisively. The restaurant for the oil company Petrofina in Leopoldswijk in Brussels (1994-1995) is a good example of this. This is an urban block in which an inner section was to become an area for the use of the staff. Samyn chose to build an elegant traversing glazed roof between the two rear facades. The theme of this design is Samyn's zeal to construct glazed roofs where the border between indoors and outdoors blurs.

HARMONIC STRUCTURES

Just as at its inception, the Samyn practice has remained permanently preoccupied with theoretical research into structural applications. Samyn's participation in congresses and his various publications treat aspects of spatial

Headquarters SmithKline Beecham Biological, Rixensart, invitational competition, 1996

structures. This study work gives him and his assisting engineers that extra motivation in their constant search to enhance logical construction methods.

Tridimensional trusses developed since 1950 are based on the truss morphology, with three bars in the form of a half-hexagon. However, the study of truss morphology optimization remains limited. The number of parameters to take into account are numerous even when considering a single isostatic horizontal straight truss beam loaded vertically and uniformly. The harmonic structures that have been developed by Samyn and Partners since 1989 are based on trusses with variable mesh sizes.[20] Harmonic structures may be defined as any truss (being straight or curved beams, with parallel or non-parallel upper and lower chords, tridimensional flat or curved trusses with parallel or non-parallel upper and lower surfaces), with a variable mesh size. The first study (1992) on a straight isostatic truss beam where mesh sizes followed the terms of a "Fibonacci" series showed that it could be lighter than the corresponding Warren truss with a constant mesh size. Some harmonic truss beams with meshes following a geometric progression are interesting alternatives to Warren beams within a slenderness ratio of 5 to 16.

Samyn's research into these structures has run in parallel with the evolution of new possibilities for their realization: "The widespread use of robots and programmable machine tools in the steel construction industry currently permits an economic realization of flat or three-dimensional lattice beams in which all the bars and nodes are different. Since then, it has been interesting to examine the variation in grid sizes of a lattice beam or layer to try to dispose the bars in the best possible fashion according to the variation of the shear stress and the bending moment".[21] Samyn continues his theoretical research together with the engineer Pierre Latteur, both via publications and a doctoral thesis.

This study work is pioneering and already enjoys international recognition. These harmonic structures were used in a glazed pedestrian bridge in the Heizel project (1997) and in the proposal for a pedestrian bridge in Kortrijk (1997) – designs that have been included in the project descriptions in this book.

Conceiving a form derived from a purely theoretical study is hence a logical consequence of Samyn's research into structures. His design for a small museum of wooden musical instruments, the Hobo project in Westouter (1991), arose from this very perspective. Its basic form is the oval around a heptagon and the development of spherical segments. This highly theoretical project for a wooden construction is very significant in terms of his vision, which he himself describes as "the immutable value of geometrical base forms with their obvious purity".[22] No plans were drawn up for the design; there are only schematic design drawings and a model. The model stage is important for Samyn in his development of a powerful conceptual vision.

I have already mentioned that, within geometry, the introduction of symmetry constitutes the organizational beginning. Buildings that have an asymmetrical layout are rarely seen within the oeuvre. In compositional terms, everything is geared towards the clarity of the layout. Asymmetry is avoided since it would introduce a disturbing element in the effort towards achieving calm and balance in the architecture. In Samyn's recent work, there has been an interesting development in the potential to broaden the limits of geometry. The first indication in this direction was in the design for the bio-pharmacological research centre for SmithKline Beecham in Rixensart in 1994-1995 (unbuilt). At first sight, the design for the Seghers Engineering extension (1997) seems to contain a strict symmetry. The depar-

Office building Seghers Engineering "'t Hoofd", extension, Klein-Willebroek, 1997-
Drawing and composition of the plan with geometric structure

Oval parking facility for 800 cars / SmithKline Beecham
Rixensart, 1996-2000, axonometric drawing

ture point is to revolve two rectangles of different lengths within a heptagon. This means that, within the construction, there is a repetition of identical parts. This configuration gives the plan's form an unexpected dynamism of movement which even gives rise to a "clear labyrinthine" character. This idea offers further interesting advantages, such as longer façade surfaces on the building exterior than in the inner patio. The "star-shaped" plan simultaneously reminds one of the basic form of a fortification. This design exhibits an intensive preoccupation with geometry.

The fact that Samyn and his team are able to produce very inventive solutions when asked to design civil architecture need come as no surprise. They are on a crusade seeking the clearest and most obvious layout structures without losing sight of aesthetics. Bridges as well as parking garages form almost ideal commissions to which a strict structural logic can be applied in deriving purposeful constructions.

The elliptical shape of the parking garage for SmithKline Beecham at Rixensart (1996), which is now under construction, offers a good example of this research into constructional clarity. The commission is for a free-standing construction providing parking facilities for 800 cars. The ellipse does not just produce a powerful building with a continuous traversing façade, it also creates a flowing gyratory movement in the parking garage that spirals upward. The layout consists of long T-shaped beams, all of the same length and section. In the prototype, the stairwells and the lifts were located in the centre. In a later design refinement, the stairs were relocated into two outer corners. This improves both the design's purity and stability.

With his large glazed dome for the "Wallonia Forestry Centre" at Marche-en-Famenne (1992-1995), Samyn has already demonstrated that wood can be used in an inventive fashion. This is the project that is featured on the cover of this book. Wood is a significant raw material in Wallonia and according to Samyn, could be put to much more inventive use. Based on this perspective, Samyn developed a prototype for a 500-space parking garage on a site on the university campus at Sart Tilman near Liège (1997). But there's more to this than the mere choice of the raw material; with two horizontal and straight outside edges and inverted sinusoidal inside edges, the skewed floors exclusively composed of straight beams weave into each other from half level to half level. This produces permanent movement within the shape of an "eight" which generates a result that is surprising both in terms of its constructional and visual properties. Dynamic line movement permeates the object by dint of the construction and not from any formal requirement. Instead of designing parking garages with split levels, which necessitates the incorporation of an unattractive bend in the beams and is expensive, Samyn designed a continuous movement. While many an architect aims to introduce greater dynamism into spaces based on highly abstract and theoretical considerations, Samyn successfully demonstrates that research into spatial structures forms an approach that offers potential in addition to a logical construction method.

Recently, he has been investigating the potential offered by wood technology. For the large roof of the Heizel exhibition building, light wooden rafters were developed that were eventually omitted in the final version. In 1996, the Samyn practice took part in a competition to design an entirely wooden office building at Marloie. Samyn describes this proposal as a "manifesto for building using Walloon timber".

A project that has been the subject of intensive research in the last two years is the Erasmus subway station on the

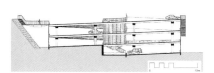

Parking facility with a completely wooden structure, University of Liège, Centre Hospitalier universitaire du Sart-Tilman, 1997, model and drawing

Carpentry workshop "Pro-Jet" for Mr. Gubin, Braine-le-Château, preliminary design, 1992-1993

Brugge farm, Marloie, bidding competition for an office building in wood, 1996

campus of the Brussels Free University (ULB). This station is a terminus and is actually above ground, and a building fabric has been used in its construction. A plastic membrane that allows the passage of light through it has been fixed onto very elegant rafters in the form of a candelabra, which is supported at four points on the station platform. The wave-like side walls are made of woven inox material. The time between the awarding of the commission and its construction has been used to maximum benefit, with the concept behind the solution being improved over time. It is clear from the drawings that considerable attention has been paid to designing the shape of the membrane's underside since this is the first part of the structure seen on riding the elevators to access the platforms.

There is absolutely no doubt that Samyn & Partners have become pioneers among architectural design practices in Belgium during the nineties. Their work possesses a coherent line, and they can take their place alongside the best of European practices striving to achieve exciting buildings by exploiting the latest technical possibilities. The contribution this Belgian practice is making towards the development of more environmentally friendly architecture, without neglecting other aspects, is also relevant in terms of the direction of contemporary architecture.

FOOTNOTES

1 Rodolfo Machado, Rodolphe el-Khoury, Monolithic Architecture, Munich - New York, 1996. First published on the
   occasion of the exhibition of Monolithic Architecture, held at The Heinz Architectural Center, Pittsburgh.
2 Tony Robbin, Engineering a New Architecture, New Haven - London, 1996.
3 L'Arca Edizioni
   Jacopo della Fontana, Samyn and Partners / Architecture to be lived, Milano, 1997.
   Lucia Bisi, Clara Wick, Elena Cardani, e.a. Philippe Samyn, L'Arca Plus, nr. 17, Milano, 1998.
4 In 1993 Samyn was invited to take part in two architectural design competitions: 1. the Neanderthal Museum at Erkrath
   (Germany / 1993); 2. a pedestrian bridge in Gloucestershire (England / 1993).
   Samyn also participated in the international competition for the design of the Nara Convention Hall (Japan / 1991).
5 Meier dropped out of the competition in the early stages and was replaced by Emilio Ambasz.
6 Marcus Binney, Airport Builders, London, 1999.
7 Jacques Aron, Patrick Burniat, Pierre Puttemans, L'Architecture Contemporaine en Belgique, Guide / De Hedendaagse
   Architectuur in België, Gids / Contemporary Architecture in Belgium, a Guide, Bruxelles, 1996.
8 Geert Bekaert, Contemporary Architecture in Belgium, Tielt, 1995.
9 Pierre Loze, Démarche: Samyn & Partners, A Plus, nr. 139, 1996.
10 Kenneth Frampton, Modern Architecture. A Critical History, London, 1985.
11 Pierre Loze, Démarche: Samyn & Partners, A Plus, nr. 139, 1996.
12 Pierre Loze, Patrick Mayot-Coiffard, Les carnets d'architecture contemporaine / Philippe Samyn: maquettes, Brussel, 1997.
13 Philippe Samyn, Laboratoire central de Solvay: construction de la maquette, March 1988. An unpublished text in which
   various aspects of the architectural model are described. The Solvay model was produced in conjunction with the workshop of the scale model maker Yvan Gilbert.
14 In the sixties, Yves Lepère worked in Louis I. Kahn's practice.
15 Horst Berger, Light Structures, Structures of Light / The art and engineering of tensile architecture, Basel, Boston, Berlin, 1996.
16 Tony Robbin, Engineering a New Architecture, New Haven & London, 1996, p. 23.
17 Hans-Joachim Schock, Soft Shells, Design and technology of tensile architecture, Basel, Boston, Berlin, 1997.
   Klaus Daniels, Technologie des ökologischen Bauens, Basel, Boston, Berlin, 1995.
18 Marc Dubois, OCAS gebouw te Zelzate, in: S/AM, nr. 2, 1992.
19 Revue Trends / Tendances, Election of the building of the year, 1997.
20 Philippe Samyn & Laurent Kaisin, Harmonic Structures: the case of an isostatic truss beam, 1992.
   Philippe Samyn & Pierre Latteur, Displacements of Structures / Application to classical structures, 1998.
   Philippe Samyn & Pierre Latteur & John Van Vooren, Volume of Structures / Application to classical and harmonic
   structures, 1998.
21 Philippe Samyn, Fractals and Harmonic Structures, in: Samyn and Partners / Architecture to be lived, Milano, 1997.
22 Pierre Loze, Samyn & Partners, in: A Plus, nr. 115, 1992.

The plot of land for the building is located on the edge of Brussels and is surrounded by a green and wooded residential area. The client wanted an office building which could be used flexibly by various professions. Given the topography and measurements of the site, a circular plan was chosen. This basic round form gives the building considerable autonomy, resembling a large garden pavilion with neither a front nor rear side. The circle is divided into 21 segments, five of which constitute the access area. The entrance, which is entirely glazed, incorporates brick walls on either side that follow a stepped pattern. The walls follow the same direction as the segments themselves. Fir has been used for the structure, while the interior and exterior joinery has been carried out in dark red méranti. The building comprises three storeys. There is also a floor beneath ground level which contains the mechanical rooms and the sanitary facilities. A central hall forms the heart of the building. It forms a cylindrical space around which three staircases curve, providing access to the higher levels. The stairways also act as a transverse stabiliser for the wooden columns. Above the entrance, on the second floor, there is a circular meeting room. The ceiling of the entrance hall includes a round opening which creates a visual link with the light dome on the roof's peak. Here, a classical theme has been borrowed from the Baroque era: the central skylight terminates the space.

The roof is covered in a layer of copper-zinc titanium and is majestically crowned with a special inox weather-vane designed by the sculptor Olivier Strebelle.

The structured nature of the building and the pronounced overhang of the eaves lend the entire construction a strong Eastern flavour. It may not be just a coincidence that the design was conceived following a trip to Istanbul, a city with major buildings of a monumental nature and a multiplicity of wooden constructions.

We can also regard the building as a giant piece of furniture that has been carefully designed right down to the smallest of details. It is a project that demonstrates the architect's fascination with wood as a construction material; he is on a journey of exploration that later leads him to design his frontier-breaking building at Marche-en-Famenne. Whilst the main concern in the design of the Boulanger office building is the creation of a solid construction, the smaller wooden details derive from an interest in using the tiniest wooden sections.

Client:
Eric Boulanger
1988-1990

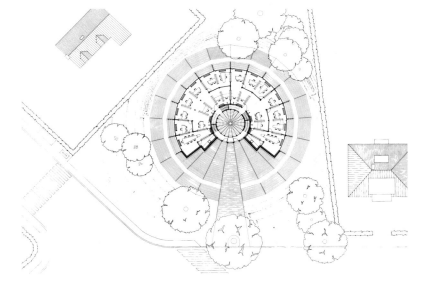

Site plan

Exterior view of the office side

Exterior view of the entrance side

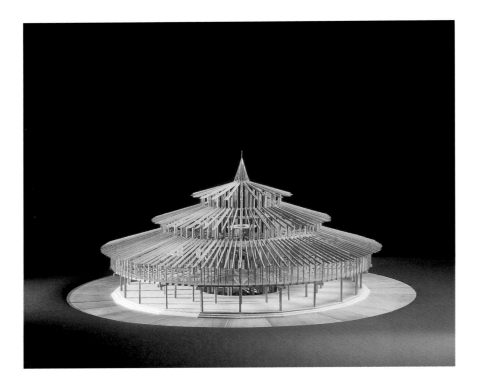

Structural model

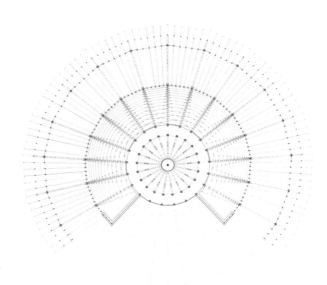

Plan of typical floor structure

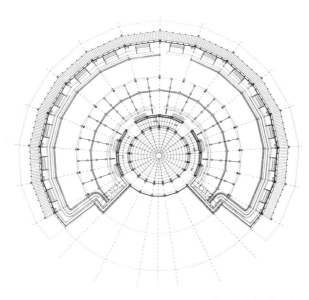

Plan of mechanical equipment

Meeting room on second level

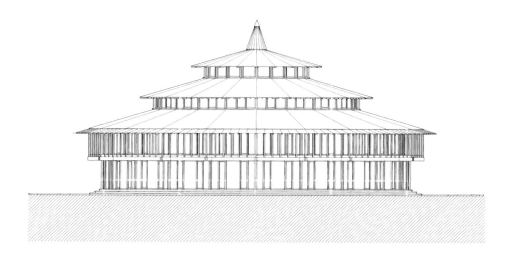

Elevation

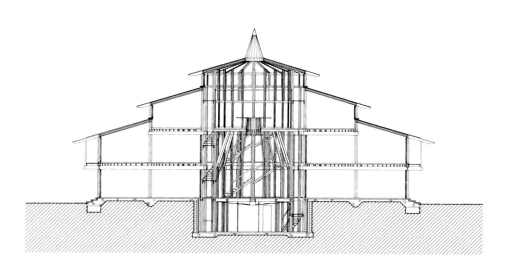

Section

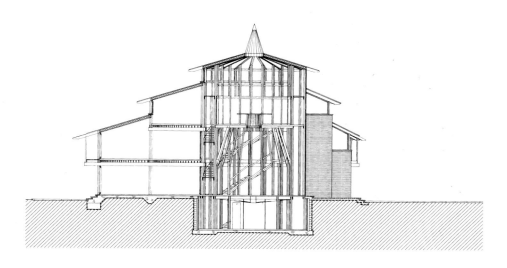

Section

Interior view of the first level

Interior view of the first level

BRUSSIMMO OFFICE BUILDING | Brussels, Belgium

The building is located in Leopoldswijk, a district of Brussels in which a large number of European institutions have their headquarters. The siting of the construction (48 x 18 metres) is such that it has two street fronts. It was at the end of the eighties that the Samyn practice worked on a series of designs based around a double frontage (BBL, Solvay and Euroclear projects).

The Brussimmo project was the first they built based on the central theme of a double skin. At first glance, this requirement seems to have been solved using a traditional cavity wall solution, but its actual realization is far more complex than this suggests. A double skin solution was chosen due to the considerable noise pollution at the site's location as well as the decision to use as bright a glass as possible in the construction. Thus far, however, there remains the problem of the warmth of the sun on the building. The cavity is used as a drainage channel for the air departing the climatically controlled offices. The air is drawn via the plenum into the cavity where it is transported up to the top storey of the building in which the mechanical equipment is situated. It was decided to utilize sunshading inside the offices so that the air flow in the cavity would not be disturbed. The cavity itself is almost one metre across, which permits proper cleaning of all the glass surfaces; ease of maintenance was another factor taken into consideration in the building's design. Another reason for the wide cavity is the idea of including light stairways as a secondary means of communication within the building. We can already see this solution in the project's preliminary model.

The outer façade has been constructed in metal and glass, while the inner façade is in glass and wood. It is the choice of wood in particular that lends the interior of the building its unusual character since wood is not generally to be found in traditional office buildings.

The character of the building is somewhat classical, given the presence of a prominent base and the pronounced conclusion of the roof. The semi-cylindrical roofing vault is closed and contains the mechanical equipment as well as an imposing conference or reception room that features a wide view out over the town. A series of fourteen ventilationducts offers a visual link between the frontage and the roofing vault. This transitional zone was absent from the preliminary design stage. At the same time, the roof vault was seen as an entirely glazed structure.

The floor plans shows a remarkable clarity. Each storey has a 780 m² surface area for offices which can be divided up extremely flexibly. An imaginative sewerage system was also conceived so as to offer the opportunity in the future for wet cells to be moved following tenants' wishes. Across the entire concrete floor surfaces on the various storeys channels were left and into these channels two pipes were let in. This concept allows major freedom in apportioning the office space, the like of which is rare in offices.

The strength of Samyn's approach lies in his commitment to search for technical solutions, without allowing technology to dominate the final visual picture. The Brussimmo Office Building offers a very clear illustration of this approach.

Client:
Brussimmo
1989-1993

Model view from above

The building emerging from the urban landscape

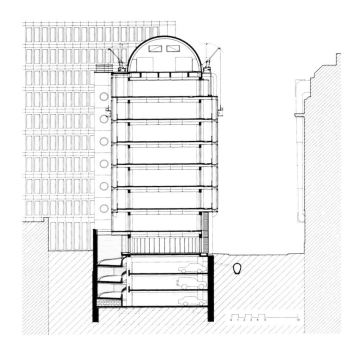

Cross-section

Perspective

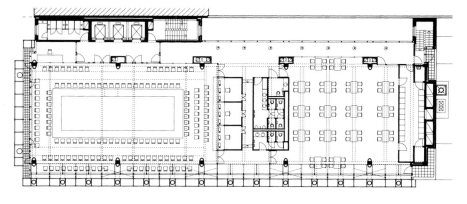

Top floor

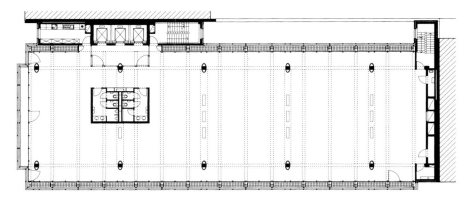

Typical office floor furnished

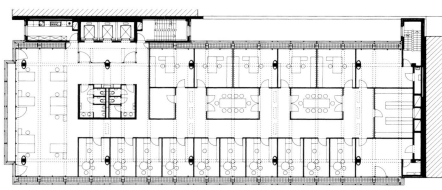

Typical office floor unfurnished

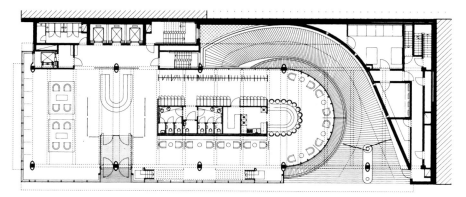

Ground floor

Meeting room under the vaulted roof on top floor

Staircase connecting the ground and first floors

Same staircase seen from the street

DUPUIS PUBLISHING HOUSE HEADQUARTERS I Marcinelle, Belgium

In designing this office building for the Dupuis publishing house, the architect was obliged to take into account a series of specific considerations. Whilst these restricted the architect, he was able to turn them to his advantage in designing a very clean concept and boosting the elegance of the volume. There was already a large new storage shed present on the building site which served as a distribution centre. The new office section was positioned in front of the architecturally uninteresting shed in the manner of a large screen. In order to retain access to the distribution centre for heavy lorries, the office volume was mounted atop tall, slender columns. This visually separates the building from the ground beneath, while the beam form is specially emphasized through the inclusion of a continuous roof edge. The three glazed volumes on the roof present an exterior reflection of the building's interior structure. Only the central patio extends down to ground level. It includes a spiral stairway and a lift. The various offices forming the administrative and creative heart of the business are grouped around the two larger lateral patios. The ground floor has been left entirely open with the sole exception of the bay in its centre where the entrance is located.

Like the Brussimmo project in Brussels, a glass surface of the greatest possible transparency was chosen for the Dupuis headquarters. Further parallels exist, such as the use of a double skin. The difference is that the patios in the Dupuis building form an integral part of the concept of the double skin. There is a separate air conditioning system in the offices in which the air is drawn off via the remaining space. This solution provides a good standard of air conditioning, despite the extensive use of glass in the construction.

The building was designed to house around 70 - 80 people. Considerable care was lavished on every detail of the interior. The design of an ingenious wooden profile for the interior walls permits a whole variety of options in their placement. This flexible solution in the arrangement of the office space was accorded a high level of priority throughout the office building design process. The walls dividing the offices from the patio are made of glass which has been placed in wooden profiling. This enhances the building's transparency. The choice of metal exterior joinery and wooden interior joinery emphazises the idea of the separation of the shell and the contents. The inclusion of the three patios lends the construction a large degree of openness for an office building. A feeling of serenity also pervades the building. It is a work in which Samyn proves that it is possible to incorporate modern air conditioning and technical materials while simultaneously creating a restrained architectural image.

Client:

Dupuis Publishing

1993-1995

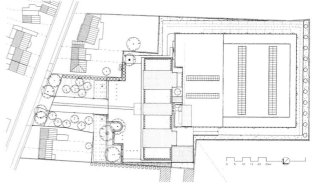

Site plan

Vertical rhythm of the horizontally shaped front façade

View of entrance façade

Entrance

Lateral façade with blinds fully open

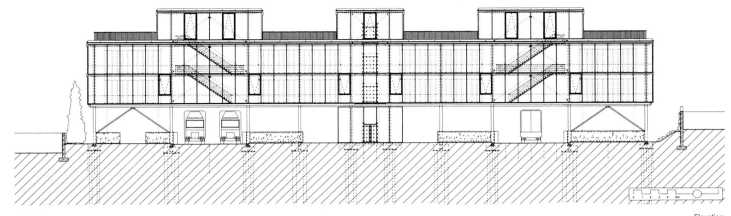

Elevation

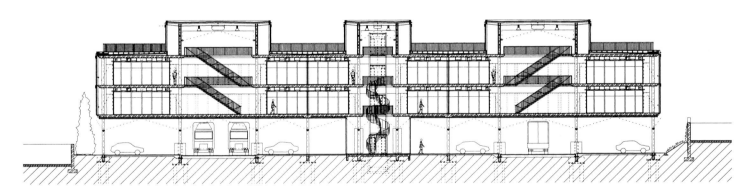

Longitudinal section

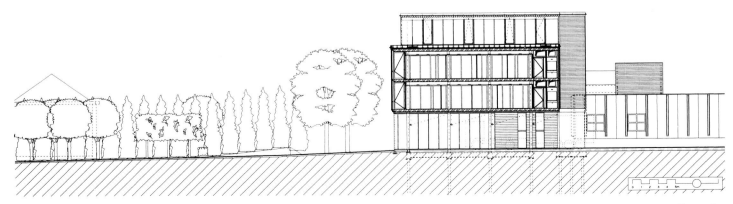

Cross-section

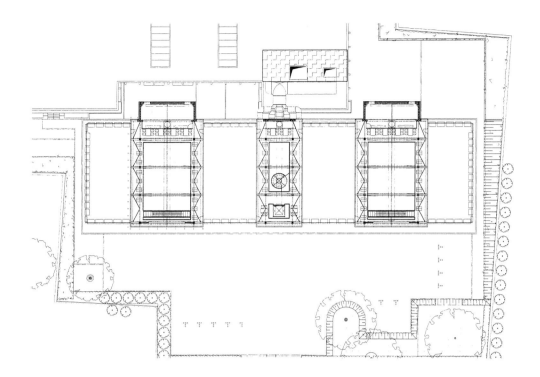

Roof floor

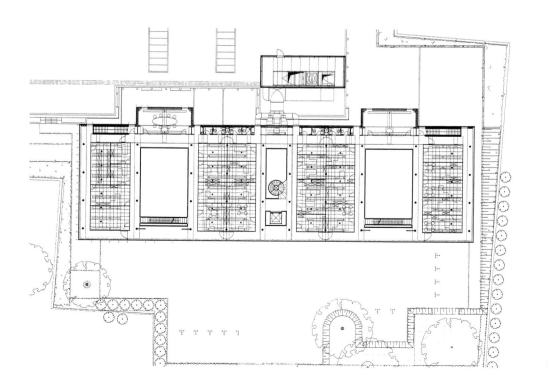

Second floor

Offices open on the atrium, which in turn opens onto greenery

Longitudinal access gallery

View of atrium with staircase

Lateral access gallery

The client's brief was to design a special office building for an isolated site surrounded by green countryside. The desired building was to be a stately country house in the Palladian style, an office building constructed in stone aspiring to be a grand country manor. In terms of the interior, the brief stated that the atmosphere should permit a tranquil and peaceful working environment, an aspect considered important by the client so that its work as a financial management centre would function properly.

An initial brief acquaintance with the project did not suggest that reversion to an existing building typology would offer an interesting approach. The eventual design of this "office villa" represents far more than just a realization of the client's vision or brief. It is also a challenging search for a solution that translates the austerity of the classical building style into something contemporary. The modesty of the concept stands diametrically opposed to the regularly propounded vision that the dynamism of a company should be reflected in a multiplicity of moving forms. According to the architect, the choice of deriving a restrained new architecture out of the classical tradition centres around the task of a comprehensive investigation into the integration of new technologies and materials.

The project consists of two parts. A small, symmetrical construction, which houses the concierge's dwelling, has a similar function to a castle's portal. A straight path leads visitors to the main entrance which incorporates a large glass surface and is emphasized by a particularly finely detailed canopy. At the rear, the symmetry is enhanced by the semi-circular extension, a form that serves to accentuate the large meeting room.

The classical character of the building is not only the result of its symmetrical construction, but also derives from the use of the square as the basic form in the floor plan. This strict order is also present in the interior. The entrance area takes the form of a two-storey-high white room in which works of art are presented, almost in the manner of a museum. This imposing part of the interior remains undisturbed by stairs, which are placed in two separate glazed zones to the side of this entrance space. The office building has a total surface area 2,603 m^2, with an additional area in excess of 1,000 m^2 comprising an underground car park and a mechanical room.

This is a project that has been finished to a high level. A variety of techniques have been used to raise the standard of both comfort and functionality, as well as to produce a serene design. Rather than constructing a stone façade, the glass manufacturer Saint-Roch co-operated in the design and created a new glazed cladding. The façade is, indeed, entirely in extraclear glass, the opaque parts being enamelled on the inside face and acid etched on the outside face. The search for new materials is not the result of a need to express a new form; rather, it represents the solution to the requirement for a white building. The architect talks of an "Emalite pierre de France". Further, the detailing of the window profiles and the interior joinery are both witnesses of a considerable technical achievement and a continuous striving towards perfection in the finish, which have demanded major commitment from both the designer and the technical specialist.

Client:
CNP-NPM
Compagnie Nationale à Portefeuille
1994-1997

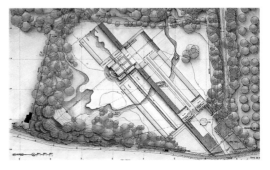

Site plan

Entrance façade

Lateral façade

The specially designed windows seen open

The large glazed canopy welcomes visitors

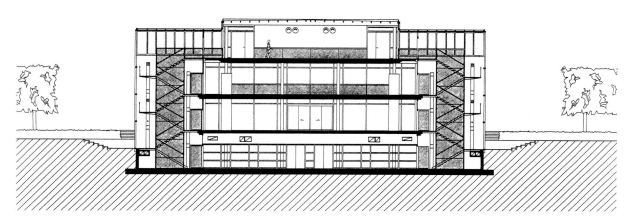

Cross-section

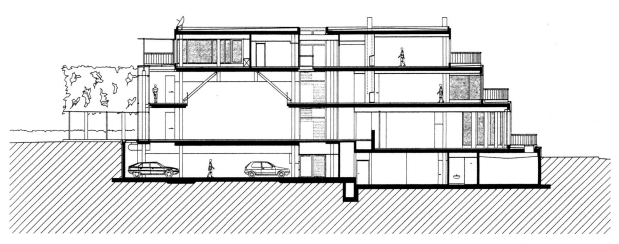

Longitudinal section

Rear façade and its mirrored image

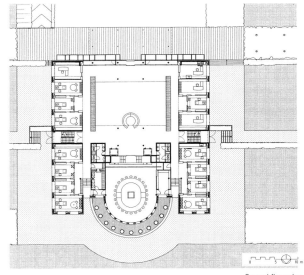

Ground floor plan

Luminous circulation area surrounded by glazed wall and roof

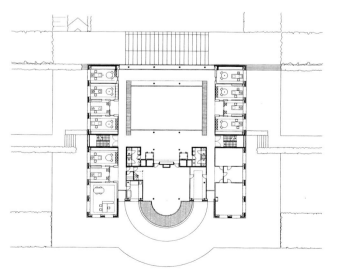

First floor plan

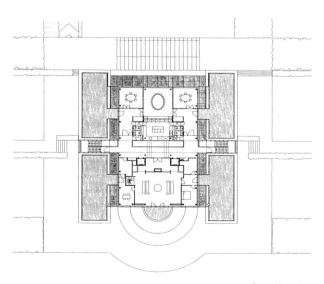

Second floor plan

First level circulation area between the front façade and the entrance lobby

Entrance lobby with glazed elevators

Meeting room

The two wings of the conciergerie connected by a glazed canopy

Entrance to the site under the glazed canopy

The Seghers company holds a leading position in Europe in the environmental technology sector. For its headquarters, it chose to occupy the former brewery Lamot, a building completed in an eclectic style back in 1911. The architect respected the structure and the character of this brick building with its neo-Romanesque arched windows and crenellations. The building's imposing character has been retained, and only the horizontal sectioning of the large windows and the slight incline in the small roof dome give a hint that there have been any interior changes. The area surrounding the complex has been landscaped with the utmost care, in co-operation with the well-known Belgian landscape architect, Jacques Wirtz.

Some of the machine parts that were formerly used in the brewery are now displayed in the interior. A new floor was constructed on every storey so as to permit a maximum of flexibility in arranging the new office landscape. The most striking new feature is the newly built link between the two volumes of the building. A glass lift shaft and an attractively detailed spiral staircase form critical elements in the tall central space. This interior patio functions not only as the building's vertical zone of circulation, but also allows daylight to penetrate right into the heart of the structure. This is a renovation that goes to show how, with a dose of creativity, solidly built industrial premises can be transformed into something fresh and meaningful. This particular project received a commendation in 1997 as one of Belgium's most interesting commercial buildings.

Given the company's major growth, it is planned to expand the building by around 5,000 m² through the addition of a newly built extension directly onto the modernized brewery section. The design plan is very enlightening when it comes to understanding the overall concept. The departure point is a strict geometry and a concentric construction. A pair of volumes, each with a rectangular floor plan, is repeated seven times in a spiral-shaped layout emanating from a central point. A look at the design plan calls to mind the pattern of a fortification, in particular due to the pointed configuration that creates a similar distortion. In order to create a link with the existing building, a transitional section has been included. The height of the building varies from two to four storeys. The structure of the façade incorporates a strict three-part vertical modulation between the columns.

This concept results in a different scale in the façades of the inner area versus those that together make up the extension's outer circumference.

The repetition of an identical core results in an exciting interior layout. Not only does this generate intermediate zones that assume a more collective demeanour, but it also offers unimagined opportunities for the routing of the corridors.

The required parking spaces are housed in an adjacent rectangular building that already existed. The upper portion of this volume contains six small workshops. This is without doubt a very exciting project in which the offices impart a monumental impression. It is a demonstration of the potential that can be derived from the strict application of geometry, while at the same time these features remain inconspicuous in the final result.

Client:
Seghers Engineering
1993-1997 (transformation)
1997- (extension)

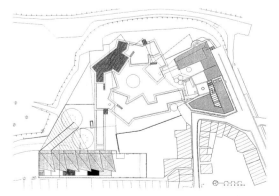

Site plan

Roof terrace

Night view of the renovated building

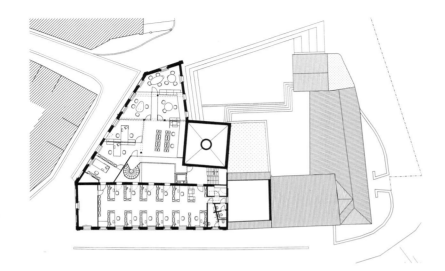

Fourth floor

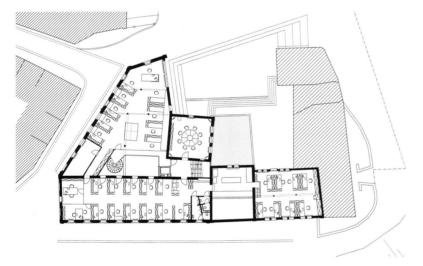

Third floor

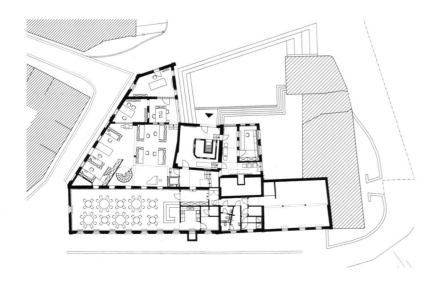

Ground floor

View of the atrium from the ground floor

View of the elevator from the staircase

View of the atrium between the staircase and the elevator

Interior view unfurnished

A delicate renovation in a typical landscape

Rear façade

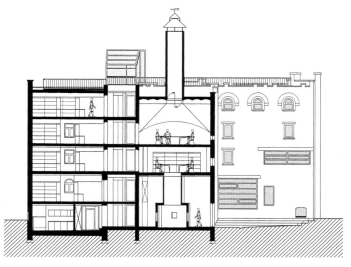

Section through the ventilation chimney

Day view of the renovated building

Section through the atrium

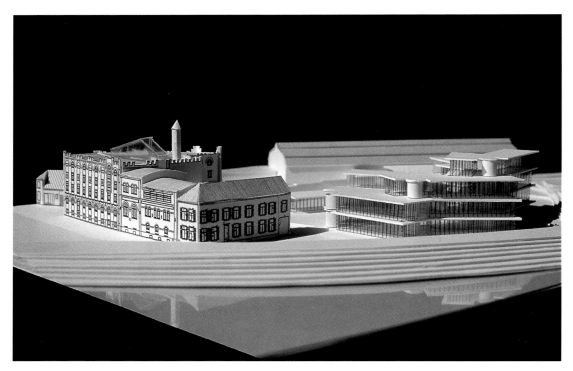

View of the model with the river in the foreground, the renovated building on the left and the planned extension on the right

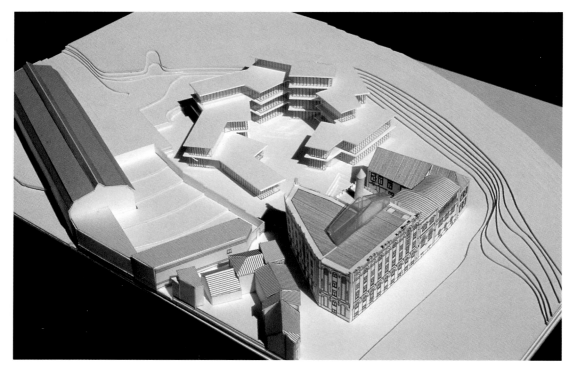

View of the existing buildings and the planned extension

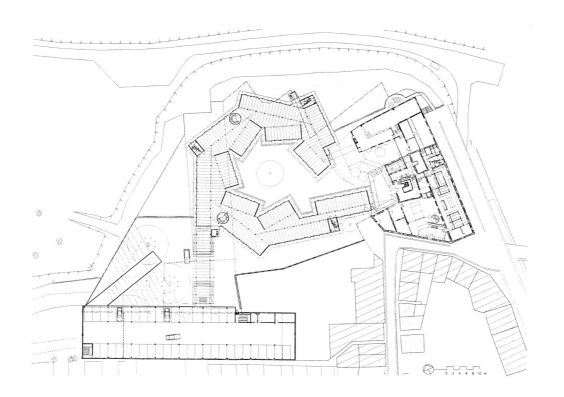

Ground floor plan

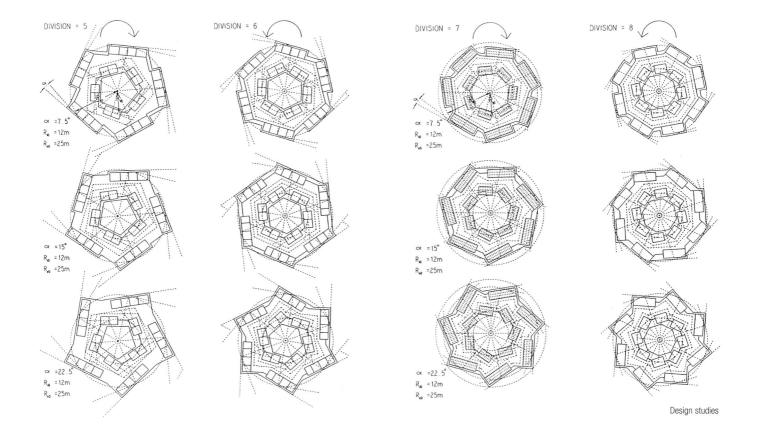

Design studies

OFFICE BUILDING "TORRE ENTEL" | Santiago, Chile

In 1993, the Samyn practice designed the Arauco Bridge, its first commission for the Chilean capital. The requirement was for an elegant cable-stayed bridge for pedestrians with a span of sixty metres. In 1997, there followed a design request on a totally different scale – the new Social Welfare Headquarters, a building which, from the outset, was intended to become a city landmark. The construction site is urban and has existing buildings on either side. The concept was for a pyramid-shaped construction, with a total surface area of 25,000 m².

The building has three levels of underground parking, a six-storey high podium, and an upper section comprising six storeys plus completely transparent tower ends. The glass façade slopes 19°. The choice of glass is meant to symbolize the openness of Chile's young democracy and the ambitious plans of this new governmental institution. However, the building also represents a further investigation into creating a building that combines transparency and energy efficiency. The external envelope is composed of a double façade with adjustable Venetian blinds. The 75-cm-wide void between the two glazed panels of the double skin is for airdraft and maintenance. The building's podium includes shadowy patios which create a natural upward circulation of air in the glazed cavity wall. The cavity functions as a solar chimney with major shifts of air.

The building is topped by a huge space that is used for a restaurant and a large inside garden. There is a sloped passage leading up to the roof from which a splendid panorama of the Andes can be seen. The top-level space has virtually the same dimensions as the large interior patio in the podium. The north façade is a huge solar panel with photovoltaic cells, integrated into the exterior glass skin, and producing enough electrical energy for the mechanical cooling units. Free cooling and natural air pull, with a complementary exchange of frigories from the 85-metre-deep water table, limit the need to install mechanical cooling units.

The organization of the floors and their supports, made out of a whole series of inclined columns contained in the architectural layout, is sufficient to ensure the stability of the wind bracing of the building even when subjected to earthquakes. The logic of the construction led to the building acquiring a solid substructure. The constructional layout consists of triangles that combine spatially to look like pyramids.

In this project, like in his other office designs, Samyn opted for a maximum of freedom in apportioning the office space. Flexibility is always accorded priority, and the designer's task focuses on finding creative solutions to this particular problem. Samyn cleverly placed the lifts in the façades as well as devising an ingenious system for the sanitary rooms. This means that the available space can be adapted to function exactly as the future occupier requires. Although we are only discussing a competition entry here, the project offers a very good insight into the practice's approach to combining aspects such as energy saving, transparency, flexibility and elegance of the designed form.

Top floor restaurant

Client:
Republic of Chile,
Ministry of Public Works
1997

Computer image of the fully glazed building

The prismatic shape of the building emerging from the surroundings

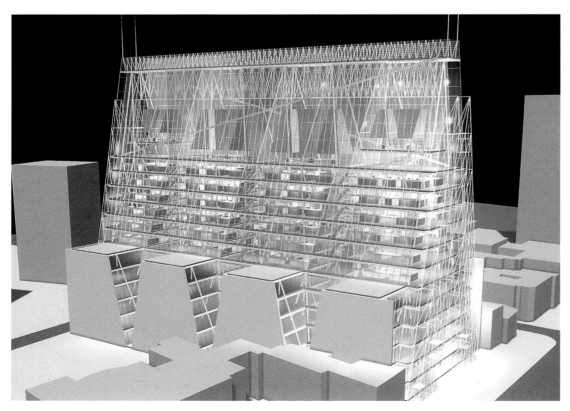

Internal combination of office floors and atria pyramids

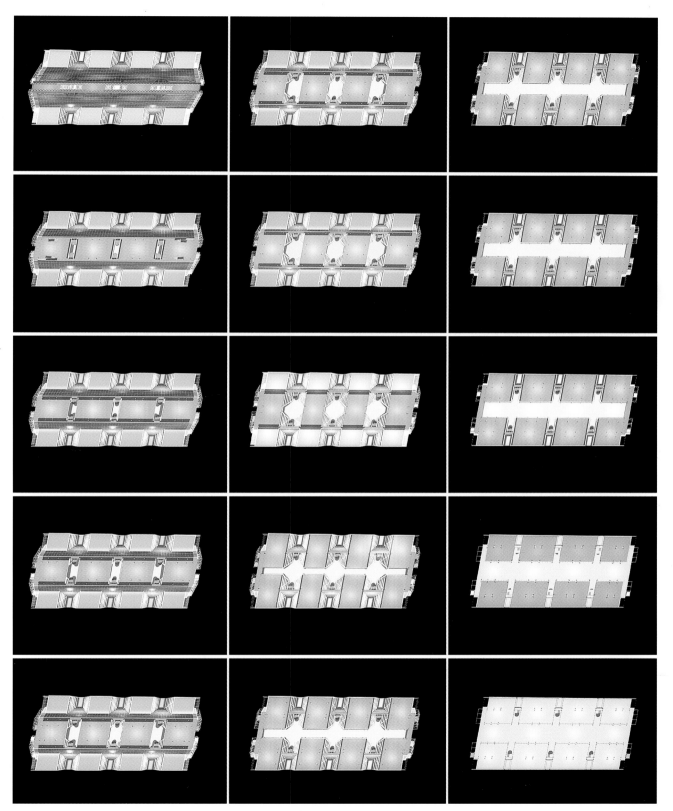

Floor plans

This project represents the first significant foreign venture by the Samyn practice. The roof structure of this inventive design uses a membrane, under which the volumes, which function as a research centre, have been placed in a free layout. The outside shell is inscribed in an almost elliptical-shaped base measuring 85 x 35 metres.

The building is located in the heart of a rectangular-shaped lake. It has two entrances - a main entrance and a small service entrance. There are also two emergency exits at the building's other extremities. The choice to locate the construction on a sheet of water, which gives rise to reflections of its elegant roof on the water's surface, is more than just for aesthetic reasons. It also gives the building an air of isolation which simultaneously renders it more secure. Furthermore, the water is also used for cooling the discrete volumes located beneath the roof membrane.

The choice of this construction method was determined by economic and climatological factors. Its extreme lightness is a positive feature when it comes to earthquakes, while the shortness of the construction time was a further significant factor. It was begun in July 1990 and was ready for occupation by the end of March 1991.

To achieve the optimum span for the roof membrane of 12 through 15 metres, it was necessary to incorporate six arches. The structure therefore includes six curved space framework girders beneath which a double curved polyester shell has been attached. The trussed arches are not parallel but radiate from a common line; they are turned to make graceful slopes with the membrane.

Length-wise, the arches are held in position with the help of six pre-stressed cables. The steel skeleton is extremely lightweight, weighing a mere 15 kg per m² of floor surface area. It consists of 1,764 pieces of tubing which takes a remarkable 411 different forms! Computer technology has been used extensively in both the design and the construction. The seven membranes, made of polyester covered in a layer of PVC, extend between the arches and the floor surface. These take the form of saddleback surfaces. The arches are covered in a curved membrane of transparent PVC. A flexible form of PVC connects the main structure and the glazed steel frames.

The large volume beneath the tent is hermetically sealed for functional and safety reasons. The interior is ventilated mechanically using pulsion and suction ventilators at the tent's extremities. This is a perfectly adequate solution for controlling the normal range of temperatures. An independent air conditioning system has been installed in the offices and laboratories for limiting their heat load. Air is both introduced and expelled via the side walls. In the interior, the window frames and other joinery have been executed in pitch pine.

This project also illustrates the fact that the designer in his capacity as an engineer has not allowed himself to be governed only by technical calculations but has also included aesthetic considerations in his design decision-making. Tony Robbin adds: "He admits to overriding engineering decisions for architectural reasons. The trussed arches, for example, are triangular in section, and a more logi-

cal engineering choice would have been to place the flat side uppermost and hang the membrane from inside the arch, attached to the inward ridge. Such a design lacks finesse; instead, Samyn rotated the triangular sections of the arch so that the roof swoops to delicate points, the membrane attaching to the flat underside. He has also understood and exploited one of the most visually rich properties of membranes". The Samyn practice worked on this membrane construction together with Harald Muhlberger of the IPL Group.

Thanks to the indirect lighting of the interior, the white canvas roof takes on a magical appearance at night.

Client:
Sinco Engineering Spa.
1989-1991

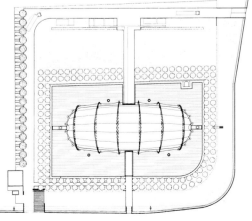

Site plan

Exterior view with the building reflected in the water

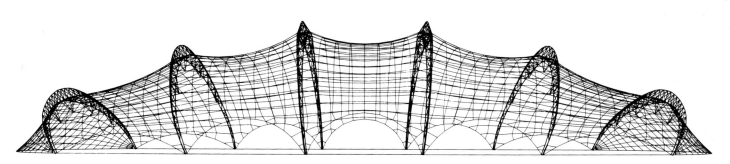

Structural diagram showing arches holding the roof membrane

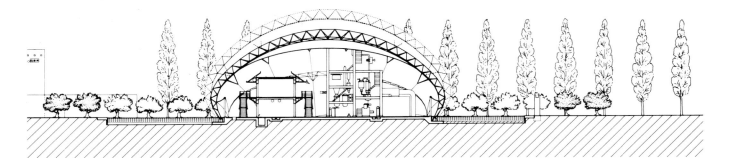

Cross-section

Model with translucent skin

Entrance

Building at dusk

Interior view with office and mechanical blocks

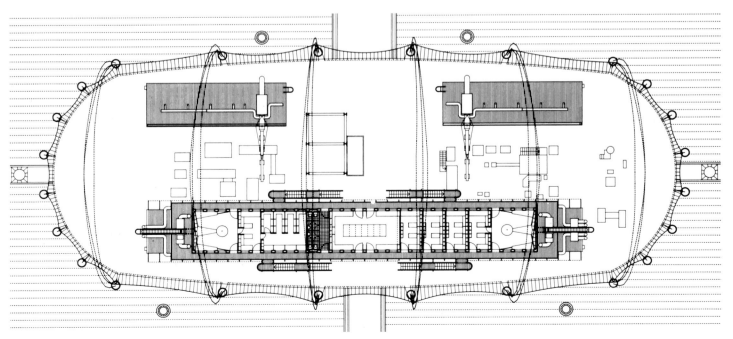

Plan showing office block

Staircase leading to offices

A gallery provides access to the offices

Detail of roof membrane with truss arch and stabilizing cables

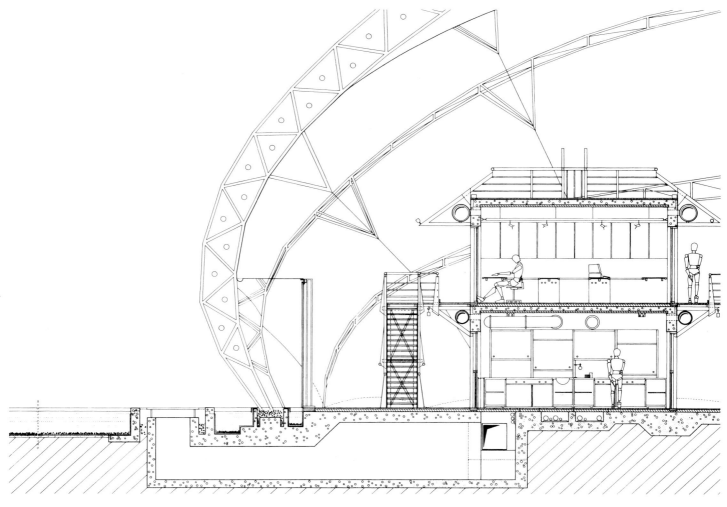

Detail section at the edge of the building

Wood manufacture is of major economic importance in the Walloon region of Belgium. Hence the Walloon government decided it would like to have a building constructed that would symbolize this dynamic sector of its industrial life. The architect was therefore asked to design a building which used wood in a highly technological way. The solution developed by the Samyn architectural practice is particularly inventive, although at first sight the end result appears to be very simple. Marche-en-Famenne, located in the midst of the Ardennes, was selected for the building's location. There were 200-year-old oak trees growing on the chosen building site.

The Centre consists of a workshop area, a group of cold-storage rooms and several offices. The workshop itself is comprised of zones for drying, stock and treatment.

The Centre's appearance is a result of the interaction between function, climatic comfort, a structural concept and the desire to create an economical structure that is low-cost and easy to maintain.

It was decided to avoid the use of rectangular volumes in the construction. This obliged Samyn to utilize the wood in the building in an ingenious fashion. The trees that grow in the Ardennes supply high-quality timber despite the fact that their diameter is small. In designing the commission as an ellipsoid, the problem arose as to how the timber could be imparted a curved shape. It was already necessary to subject the wood to a steaming process in order to kill off the insects and fungi present in it. This led to the idea of applying its curved form while it was still in the steaming chamber. This meant that the timber could be incorporated into the construction free of stress.

In the early stages of the design process, it was hoped to take advantage of the relaxation of green or untreated timber. However, this option was later rejected.

The span consists of a grid in which four different-sized beams are used (8x16, 7x14, 6x12 and 5x10 cm). What is so creative about this particular building is that the differences in the sectioning provide the opportunity of fully utilizing the beam's strength, in spite of the fact that the thickness of the composite beam remains a mere 21cm at every point.

The exterior envelope is composed of large pyrolized laminated glass tiles. The supple aluminium arches possess a "T-profile" and shore up the transversal carrying arches in order to support the 1,691 tiles placed on a silicon base.

The interior buildings are composed of concrete masonry block units so as to provide thermal mass and fire protection. They also provided a base from which to erect the principal framework of the roof at the time of its assembly. The two interior buildings support the horizontal loads from the dome structure. The buildings are each climatized separately. The roof structure uses a net wood volume of 114 m^3, covering a floor space of 960 m^2 and an interior volume of 6,510 m^3.

This particular construction is one of the Samyn practice's most interesting projects. Here, they have adopted a very novel approach to both the construction and the detailing. This merely underscores Samyn's view that, armed with considerable knowledge in construction technology, it is possible to create buildings whose form is far superior to many purely high-tech constructions.

Client: Regional Executive Walloon,
Ministry for the Environment,
Natural Resources and Agriculture,
Namur, 1992-1995

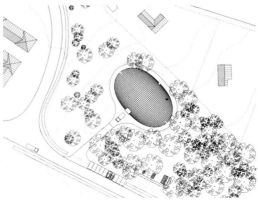

Site plan

Night view of the illuminated volume

Entrance in the middle of the curved volume

Aerial view

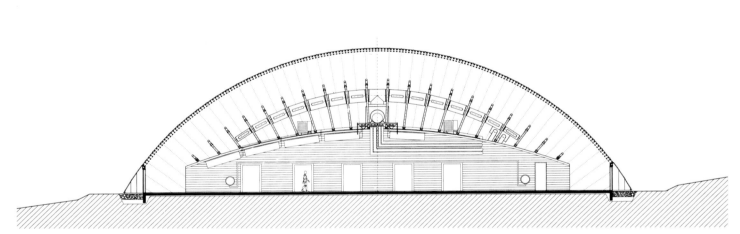

Longitudinal section showing mechanical equipment

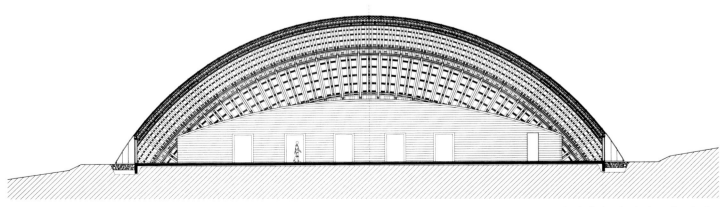

Longitudinal section showing roof construction

Lateral corridor

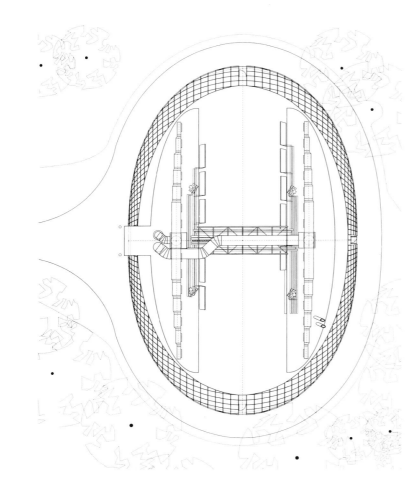

Plan of mechanical equipment above the internal blocks

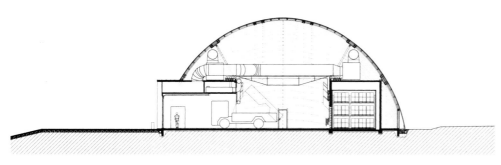

Cross-section showing mechanical equipment

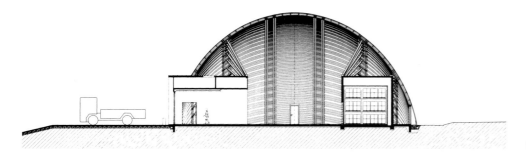

Cross-section showing roof structure

Interior view of the hall, with the internal blocks – housing offices, laboratories and cold storage spaces – flanking the "nave"

The two internal blocks serve
as additional roof support construction

Mechanical ducts between the two internal blocks

Roof construction showing wooden arches

The aim behind the OCAS (Onderzoek Centrum voor de Aanwending van Staal) project was the creation of a research centre for the investigation of new applications for steel sheets, an initiative of the steel manufacturer Sidmar, Arbed and ALZ. The design agenda foresaw offices, laboratories and large research halls. The company chose a site for the new building that was near to its head office. As the site is also very close to the intersection of two motorways (Antwerp-Knokke and Ghent-Terneuzen), the designer was very much concerned to landscape this industrial complex in as green a setting as possible. In addition, there was the requirement to design a building which would be expressive. It was intended to create a landmark which nonetheless was also capable of meeting some very specific functional requirements as far as the internal organization was concerned.

A prominent feature of the site is the lake that surrounds the building. Its circular form is 180 metres in diameter. Its banks on the north and south sides are five metres high while the west and east sides are at normal ground level. This permits four access routes: two to the entrance area which has an associated, covered parking lot, plus two to the basement of the research halls themselves.

This arrangement of the volumes was achieved by use of a distinct division of the whole. One of the volumes forms an oblong 162 metres in length and contains the offices and laboratories. It was assembled as a bridge construction. The two principal girders are composite, 6 metres in height from axis to axis of its longitudinal chords. Each principal girder rests on two supports. In the preliminary design, there was a double glass front which was omitted from the final construction. The glass front is located 1.75 metres behind each of the large composite girders. The dividing walls in the building's interior are all movable which ensures a maximum level of flexibility in apportioning the space.

The two large research halls have a parabolic roof structure which is 42 metres wide and 16.5 metres high. These halls contain a whole series of different experimental devices on large support benches. The overall space has a demeanour that is both robust and slender. The fully closed parabolic roof in profiled, rolled corrugated stainless steel sheets evokes the atmosphere of gigantic storage sheds. The feeling of elegance derives from the glazing and from the fine vertical wind protectors in the brick edge surfaces. The parabolic rafters were assembled horizontally on the building site and subsequently raised up together in a single operation. The preliminary design, as the model of the construction shows, included an open structure to the underside of the curved roof. However, as the design process progressed, this solution was rejected in favour of a form that presents a simpler, more powerful appearance. The design not only offers interesting functional possibilities, but also guarantees optimal expansion potential. The long, beamed volume has been raised to provide a section for covered open parking, offering protection against the weather. Direct access to the heart of the building is possible via this parking lot. By positioning the circulation area in the very heart of the building, the two main axes intersect one another in the middle of the upper floor; one circulation route leads to the offices while the other provides access to the research halls. The design has also minimized walking distances within the building. A more solid foundation has been built under the central hub which would allow for the construction of an 8-storey-high cylindrical tower should future expansion be warranted.

Client:

SA. Ocas (Sidmar-Arbed-Alz)

1989-1991

Aerial view

Workshop parabolic roof and office bridge

View from south-east

Glazed façade of the workshops and its mirrored image

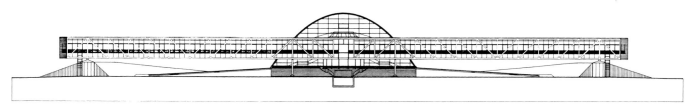

Longitudinal section

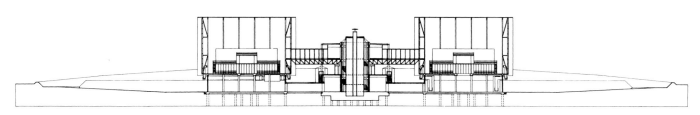

Cross-section

The steel structure under construction

Interior view of a workshop glazed façade

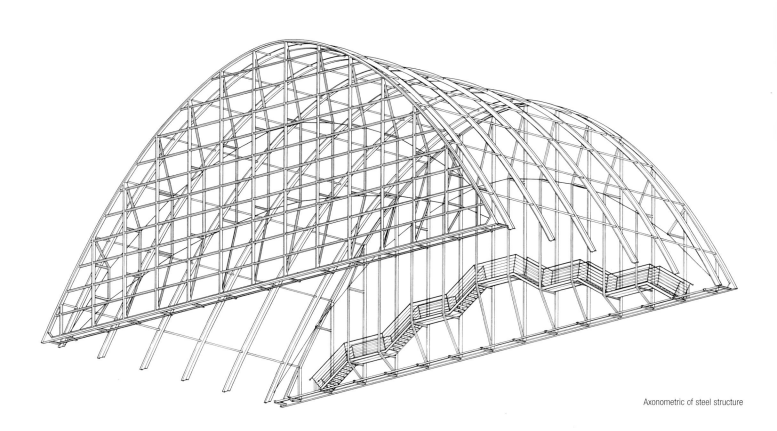

Axonometric of steel structure

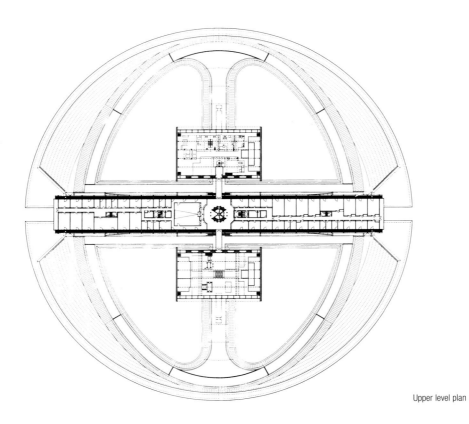

Upper level plan

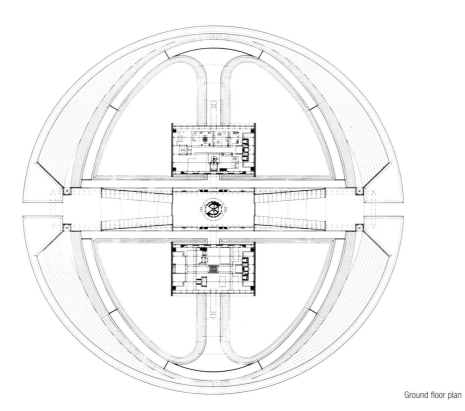

Ground floor plan

Interior view of a workshop

Loading area underneath the bridge building

The E411 motorway cuts right across the Ardennes in Belgium, connecting Brussels and the city of Luxembourg. Wanlin lies on this particular European traffic artery, in a shallow valley in the woody Famenne district. On the occasion of their 75th anniversary, Petrofina decided to develop a new generation of service stations, whereby an increase in customer comfort was the principal requirement. At the same time, they were in search of a powerful architectural image which should excite the admiration of the visitor. The aim was to create a piece of quality architecture without involving an increase in building costs.

Given this vision, the designers chose to cover the entire service station with a large canopy. However, rather than building a traditional flat canopy - the solution adopted for almost every service station – a "spherical" construction was chosen for this project. This unexpected form of service station roof fits much better into the undulating character of the landscape. All parts of the design agenda, including the shop and the sanitary services, are gathered together into a simple rectangular volume that is positioned entirely independently beneath a tent-like cover. The strictness of this glass and metal box introduces an interesting visual tension with the curved overhead canopy.

The basic form of the roof evolved out of small models made of nylon stockings, cardboard and sewing thread. A sophisticated computer program was then used to calculate the precise form, which is very much affiliated to the study models. This roof design takes into account extreme weather conditions plus the the tent-like roof's unpredictable aerodynamic behaviour. It has also been recognized that the values output by the calculation, which are very important when it comes to creating a hyperstatic structure using flexible materials, can only be approximate. A network of fine stressed cables was fixed beneath the membrane in order to prevent distortion at high wind speeds. The membrane is made from a polyester base coated with white PVC, plus a layer of acrylic on both sides. A "pre-stressed" membrane (patent Ferrari) has been chosen, given the material's bi-directionally similar resistance properties and its high life span.

The use of a membrane construction lends the entire site a very special demeanour at night. Light penetrates the membrane roof, transforming the two service stations into virtual giant beacons alongside the motorway.

The rafters were manufactured in galvanized steel. The length of the curved framework girders, which are supported on columns of reinforced concrete, is 40 and 44 metres. Their support points were placed at a height of 5.50 metres across a grid that is 20 x 15 metres. In the search for an elegant form, it was decided to taper the columns towards the top. The aim to provide as few support points as possible was based on technical considerations.

This exceptional project was awarded the Industrial Fabrics Association International Award in 1996 and won the 1997 International Prize for Textile Architecture. Furthermore, it has most certainly contributed to the fact that other European petroleum companies are increasingly paying attention to the architectural aspect in the design of their motorway service stations.

Client:
Petrofina
1994-1995

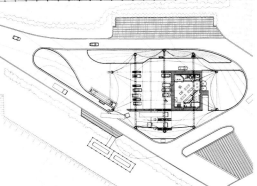

Site plan

The welcoming tent-like building at dusk

Refilling under the tent facing the shop

Rear view of the shop block located under the large umbrella

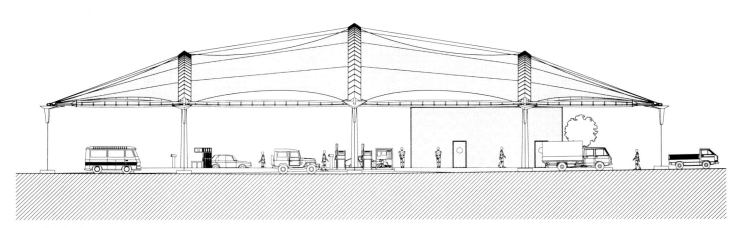

Longitudinal elevation

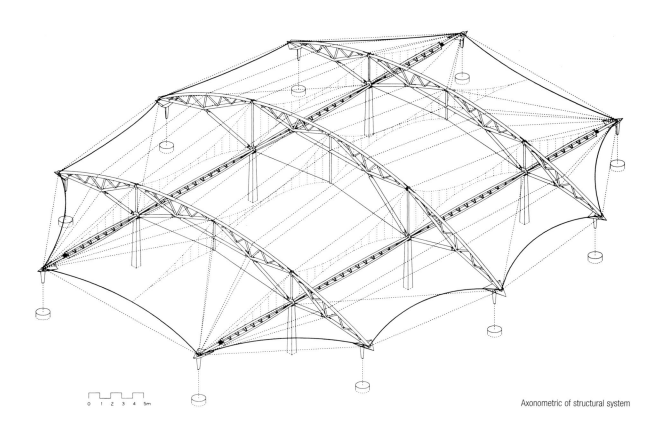

Axonometric of structural system

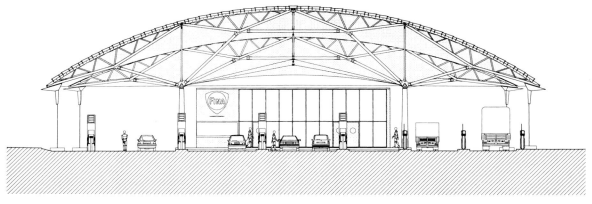

Cross-section

Roof membrane and structure

Trusses and catenaries under the roof membrane

Metal water collectors at the ends of the trusses

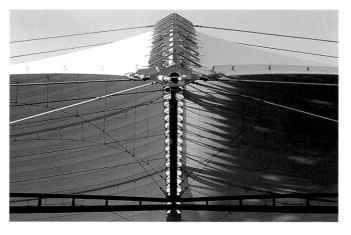

Detail of roof system

FINA PETROL STATION | Houten, The Netherlands

The oil company Petrofina commissioned this service station in their search for a new type of station to fit the framework of their "Fina 2010" programme, whose architectural aspects were defined by Samyn's team. The departure point is the creation of a style of architecture that contributes towards an increase in customer comfort and that aims to offer better, more gentle integration into both urban and rural surroundings. The new Fina station in Houten, located not far from Utrecht, is the first in a series of service stations that the Samyn practice has designed and which has been built. Following its successful Fina station at Wanlin (1995), the practice has continued its search for exciting solutions in the construction of service stations – a genre that generally adheres to a dull traditional design. The aim is to produce prominent constructions that offer an increased level of inventiveness in terms of both the concept and the construction.

One important element of a service station remains the canopy above the petrol pumps. This is often no more than a flat disc with a series of simple columns beneath. In contrast, the new Fina station incorporates a slightly sloping roof that serves to make an inviting gesture. The roof is supported by slender columns that are assembled out of four tube profiles. The form of these columns offers a direct visual link with trees, a solution that goes further than offering mere support to the roof. The solid character of the roof has been eliminated through the introduction of oblong light slits between the support points.

Service stations are very often unwelcoming places in windy conditions. The canopy in particular serves to intensify the wind strength, creating an unpleasant micro-environment. This problem has been solved in Houten by incorporating curved, galvanized steel plates with apertures comprising 50% of their surface area. Although the transparency remains limited, these wind-shields have been positioned according to the result of technical calculations and so succeed in eliminating as much wind turbulence as possible. The positioning of these metal sheets also signals the direction in which to circulate round and approach the service station.

The volume and its interior infrastructure, such as the Fina shop, are directly connected to the sloping roof. The side facing the petrol pumps is entirely glazed. The roof slope of this volume is identical to that of the large canopy. As we see from the drawings, a great deal of attention has been paid to the building's appearance after sunset. Up on the curved screens, a continuous strip in blue neon has been included. This is Fina's company colour. Having positioned the roof at an angle, the surface also works as a façade when seen from a distance. The indirect artificial light that is emitted into the darkness through the oblong apertures has a stimulating and unexpected impact.

This design is a convincing demonstration by the practice that, with the use of some imagination and creativity, it is possible to break the mould of the worn-out approach used in designing constructions of this type. As well as increasing the level of comfort, the designer has striven to make the building more expressive.

Client:
Petrofina
1998-1999

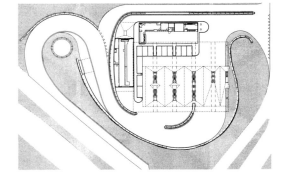

Site plan

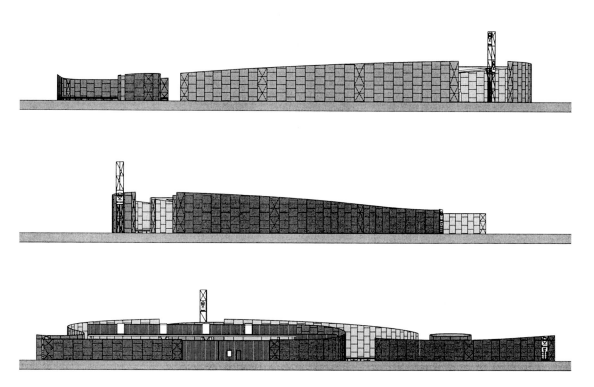

South and east front and north-west elevation

Axonometry showing the roof structure

View of steel screen

Cross-section

Day view

Perspective view of the refilling area

Cross-section

Night view

The design of the Fina service station on the motorway was received with such enthusiasm by the municipal authority in Houten (Netherlands) that they commissioned the Samyn practice to build a small fire station on a site surrounded by lots of green space. The municipality of Houten has a hybrid fire fighting force: four professional firefighters, and around sixty volunteers. The building agenda set a requirement that there should be space to accommodate six fire engines.

Samyn reverted to one of his favourite themes in drawing up the design: the radical division of the roof structure from the internal organization. It represents the idea of the shelter, the independence of the shell from the building itself. The building's interior is in keeping with the client's requirements. Samyn had already opted for this type of division in an earlier design for storehouses in Florennes, a project conducted for the Belgian Army (1991-1992). The fast method of construction was a further significant factor favouring this choice at the fundamental design stage.

The choice of a parabolic form for the roof is the result of Samyn's search for elegance of form, and also brings about an optimization of the structure. He had already demonstrated that this curved roof form presents a slender figure in the landscape in his OCAS complex at Zelzate (1989-1991).

There is a two-way split of the interior. The south side has been conceived as a completely transparent space in which just glass has been used. Here, the firefighting equipment is kept in what resembles a large shop window. This barely heated hall is intended to serve as a climatic buffer zone, both in winter and in summer. All the other functions have been gathered together in the northern half of the building, a construction built of load-bearing brickwork. From the open corridors, there is a view onto the fire engines. The ground floor houses showers, changing rooms and the sanitary provisions as well as storage rooms for mechanical equipment. There is also a meeting room and a recreation room for the firemen on the first floor. The offices are housed together on the second floor, and above these are yet more rooms of mechanical equipment.

The façade incorporates large overhead gates designed to allow the firefighting force to make a quick operational exit.

The building's length runs in an east-west direction which allows the southern façade to incorporate photovoltaic cells. The fire station's overall form appears as a modern variant on the traditional theme of the shed, a construction that is defined by the imposing presence of a large roof area.

Client:
City of Houten
1999-1999

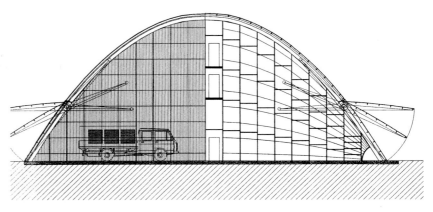

Lateral elevation

Perspective showing the closed office area and the glazed hall area

Vaulted glazed roof with photovoltaic cells

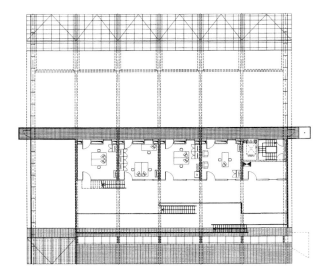

Second floor

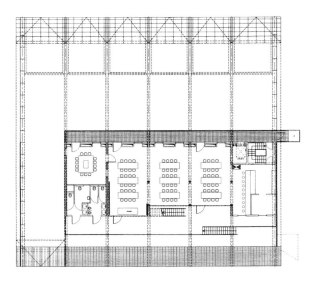

First floor

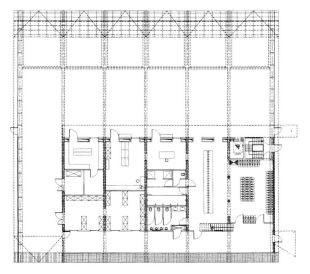

Ground floor

Computer image showing opening phases of the doors

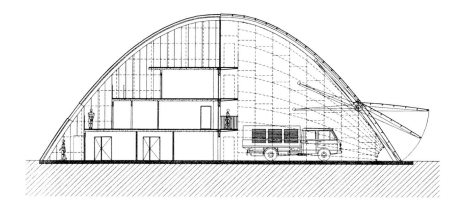

Cross-section

In 1988, the oil company Petrofina organized a competition for a fundamental re-design and expansion of their research centre in Feluy, south of Brussels. The Samyn practice was awarded this complicated commission and looked at a variety of possibilities for improving the company's internal organization. The complete surface area of the enlarged centre covers around 30,000 m².

What was significant in the complete restructure of this industrial site was the construction of a bridge spanning the Brussels-Charleroi canal. The mere building of a bridge by a private client to provide access to an industrial complex is in itself unusual enough. But this option offered the advantage of providing the public with an easy means of access to the site as well as allowing the existing pump industrial station to retain its canal-side location.

The re-design saw the transformation of what had been a disorderly pell-mell of buildings into a symmetrical configuration with clear lines. Hence the main entrance, located on the first floor, is situated along the same linear axis as the bridge. A whole series of factors have influenced the bridge's design. The obligatory unrestricted width of 49 metres above the canal, the maximum permissible slope for vehicles, and the connection with the existing road which lies some 13 metres below the bridge's access area, were all highly definitive. The level of the large access square measuring some 4,000 m² is the result of the mandatory height requirement between the water and the bridge. This generated the opportunity of creating two parking levels beneath the access square.

The concrete structure of the covered parking lot also provides the four cables of the cable-stayed bridge with the necessary anchoring mass. In this way, the deck of the bridge could be completely detached from the pylons, which also allows for the positioning of two tie back cables with dashpots for damping of the structure. The abutments, two narrow pillars, simultaneously function as a gateway offering visual access to the industrial site. The primary span is 66.39 metres, while the bridge's two smaller spans measure 26.40 and 23.10 metres respectively.

However, these are not the only notable features in the bridge's construction. Significantly, the choice of materials has allowed it to become integrated into the surrounding countryside. Both the large access square and the deck of the bridge are finished in wood, creating an interesting visual link with the landscape. The deck of the bridge is constructed from box beams with wooden boarding situated in between. The box beams also form a safety rail and provide a surface for fixing the lighting. The footpaths, likewise made of wooden boarding, have been incorporated into the overhang. The elegance of the bridge is further enhanced by the angled positioning of the balustrade.

As part of the re-design, the lighting of the bridge was given major attention. It has been incorporated in such a way as to emphasize the elegant form of the structure. This was the first bridge of Samyn's that was actually built. It is a construction in which he has sought to create a manifestation of the greatest possible slenderness.

Client:
Fina Research SA
1988-1991

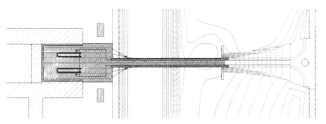

Site plan

View across the bridge towards the research centre

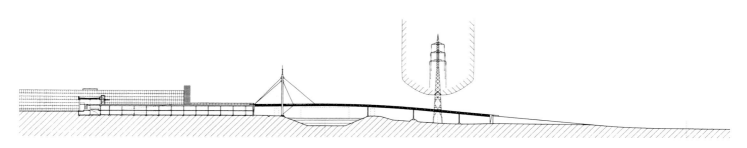

Longitudinal section of the whole project

View of bridge spanning the canal

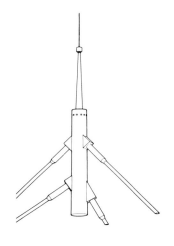

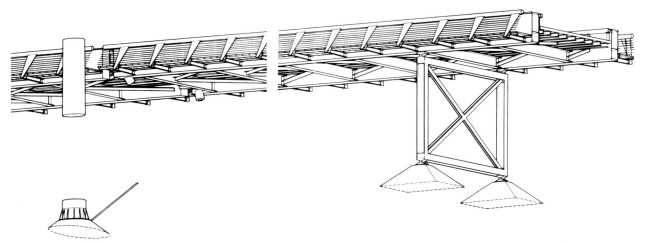

Exploded axonometric of structural components

View of the bridge and pylons

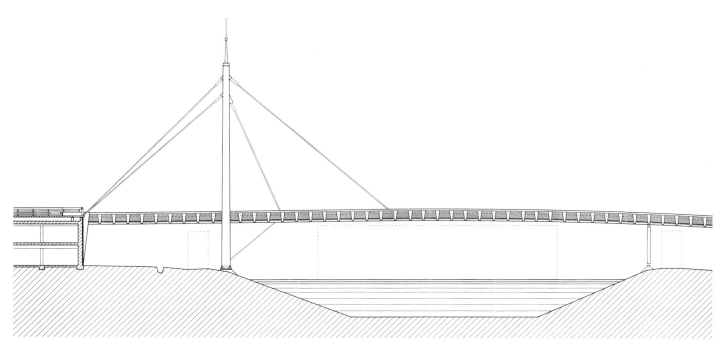

Longitudinal elevation of the bridge

In order to improve the navigability of the Leie river, its depth, and hence also its breadth, are being altered. The Leie flows through the town centre of Kortrijk and as a result, all the existing bridges are being demolished and replaced by new structures. The Samyn practice was retained to design a pedestrian bridge as one element in the overall solution. This metal bridge is extremely lightweight and spans 45 metres. An equilateral triangular cross-section of 5 m in height is more appropriate to cope with lateral loads than a rectangular one. A triangle on its base seems to be a simple solution as it allows the deck to be located at base level. For many reasons a triangle on its apex with the deck at mid-height is preferable. The transversal span of the deck is equal to the net usable width of 2.9 m, rather than spanning 5.8 m. Also the deck braces the diagonal members of the trusses at mid-height and thus reduces their buckling length by 3.

At first sight, it seems as if the bridge's design merely meets a formal requirement to introduce a flowing gesture. Its heightened level of expressivity derives from an entirely fresh approach towards spatial structures, a theme discussed in an analysis Samyn has conducted entitled "Harmonic structures".[1] This analysis demonstrates that a truss composed of isoceles triangles with a variable mesh size and internal stays can be lighter than the lightest truss referred to as a Warren truss. A truss with four meshes having a span to height ratio of nine – the two central ones being twice as wide as the lateral ones –

represents the optimum optimorum, when considering that all the external vertical forces are concentrated on the upper nodes and leaving buckling issues aside.

The transfer to the upper node of the uniformly distributed load on the deck at the mid-height of the truss, is achieved simply by an array of fanning tension rods. The buckling issues of the upper chord on the vertical plane and the hanging of the deck parts on top of the lower chords can easily be solved by curving the upper chord outwards and holding it, as well as the related deck part, with other arrays of fanning rods.

The special feature about the bridge is the small amount of material used on its underside. In one tubing profile consisting of four parts, the fan-like structures converge at one single point. Thanks to the optimal development of these combined structures, a light construction is produced which simultaneously forms an unexpected composite form. It is not only the main shape of the construction that exhibits a wave-like movement, but the deck of the bridge also slopes slightly. Whilst the breastwork on most bridges has nothing to do with their structural design, in this case the two are combined. The fundamental concept also allows a roof surface to be included to protect the bridge from the rain. This section serves to further reinforce the dynamism of the overall composition.

[1] Ph. Samyn & L. Kaisin "Harmonic Structures: The case of an isostatic truss beam".
Proceedings of the Asia-Pacific Conference on shell and spatial structures, 1996.

1998

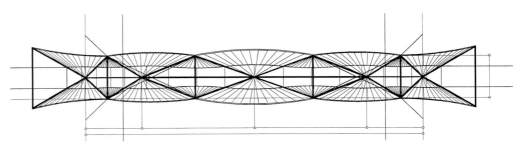

Structural plan

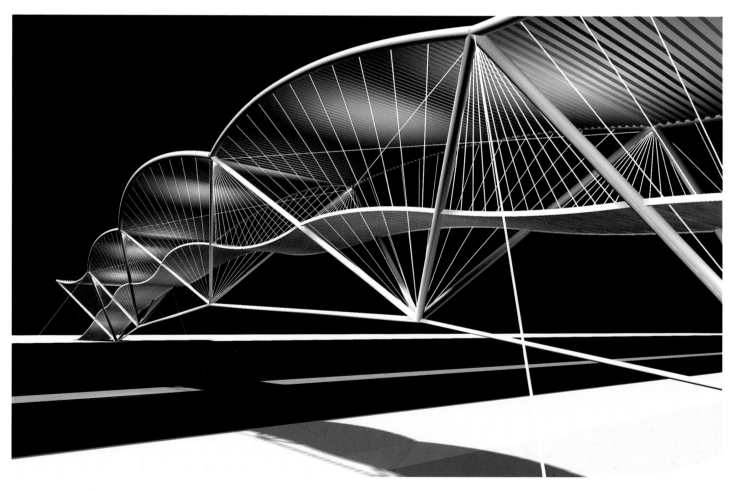

Array of fanning rods

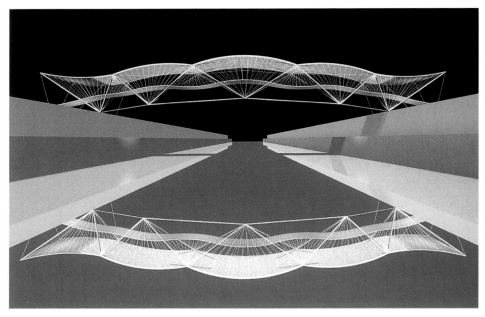

Mirrored view of the bridge in the river

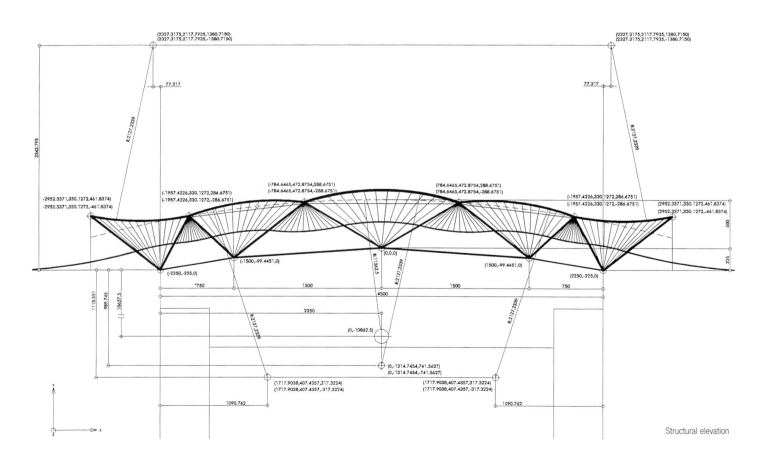

Structural elevation

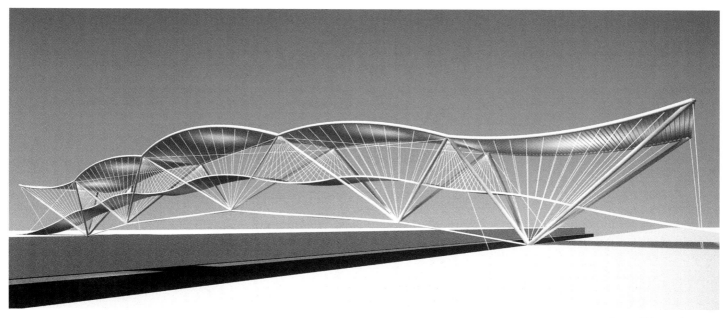

Structural lightness of the bridge

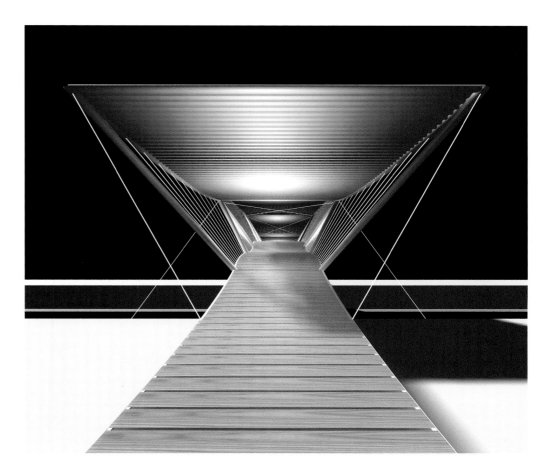

Access to the bridge

Erasmus station forms the terminus of the Brussels underground railway and is located in front of the campus of the Brussels Free University hospital.

The underground station is actually located in a raised embankment. Access is provided under the railway lines, and elevators transport passengers up to the middle of the platform. This solution and the decision to build two railway lines made it possible to limit the station's breadth to 15.30 metres. The station has a total length of 189 metres.

Right from the outset, it was chosen to use a fabric structure mounted upon steel supports. To increase the expertise they had gained on earlier projects, including a factory building in Italy and the Fina service station at Wanlin, the practice decided to use a solution that would serve to advance their knowledge. The tiny weight of such constructions is not their only advantage. Above all, they offer the opportunity of achieving an expressive form using a rationally conceived construction. Furthermore, the membrane allows the passage of light through it, and hence the interior of the building acquires an atmosphere of very diffused lighting by day. By night, the building is transformed into a giant beacon of light on the campus. Another key factor in the design is the fact that the passenger does not perceive the inner surface of the roof until he has mounted the escalator. The platform roof comprises a combination of eleven square network structures with

sides equal to 15.3 metres in length. The membranous roof is supported by twelve identical, elegant, combined rafters, each of which are borne by four supports on the platform. This integral construction, with the roof and support pillars combining to form a harmonious ensemble, merits the description of a "candelabra".

The membrane is placed over these regularly positioned rafters, resting upon a metal network. The network is automatically stable due to the membrane's curvature properties. At either end, the rafters are borne by a single column. The membrane is mounted into position using traction cables, giving the entire platform roof a high level of stability.

The type of membrane chosen is made of glass fibre coated in polytetrafluoethylene (PTFE). It weighs 1.15 kg per square metre. The side walls are made of woven inox (material woven from inox fibres). This solution offers the platform protection against the wind while retaining a certain level of transparency. The wave-like movement offers the roof its own integral stability. On first sight, the roof appears to be a simple design, while in fact, it is the result of very complex mathematical calculations to optimize its form in coping with a whole variety of extreme climatic conditions. This project is a manifestation of the Samyn practice's ambitious aim: to apply modern technological solutions and mathematical rigour to the search for elegance in the final construction.

Client: **Ministère de la Region de Bruxelles-Capital**
1997-

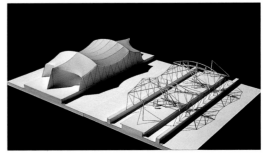

Models

View of the translucent surfaces enclosing the station

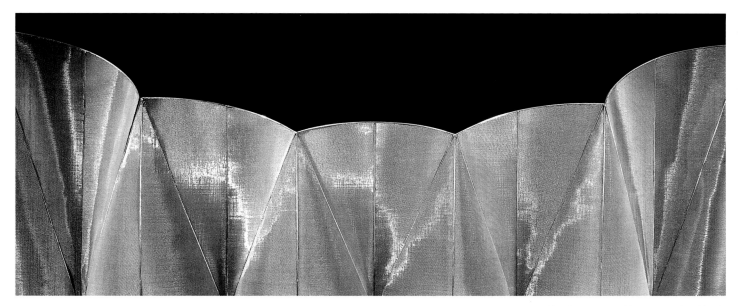

Wave-like movement of the woven inox lateral façade

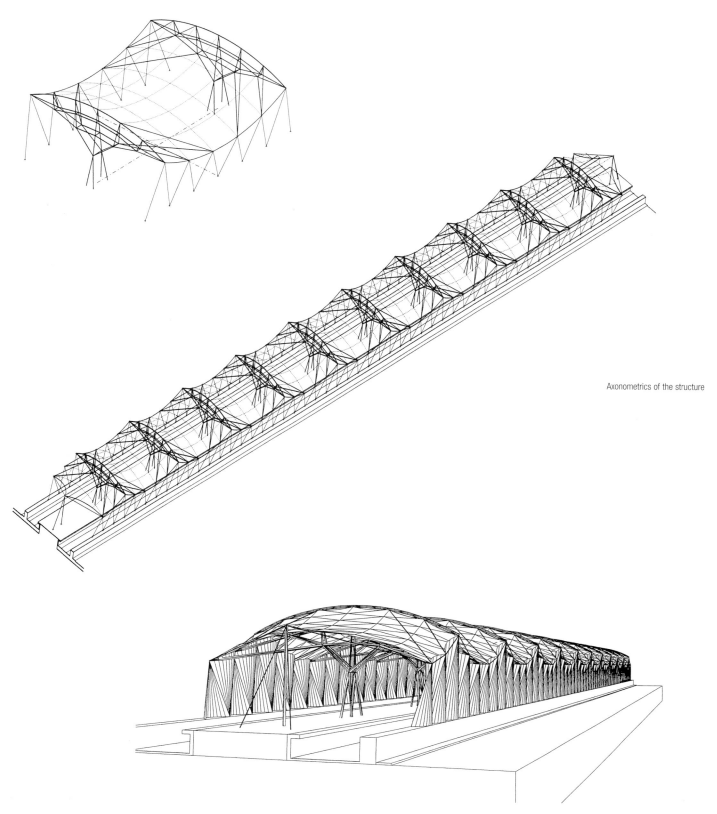

Axonometrics of the structure

General volumetric perspective

View from the central track

Roof structure seen from the ground level

The commission was for an auditorium for the medical faculty of the Brussels Free University on the campus at Anderlecht. A capacity to seat five hundred people formed part of the requirement.

A cylindrical form was chosen, both to adhere to a town planning approach and due to the specific qualities this offered for the interior. The location is surrounded by a whole series of campus buildings forming a confused picture in which no real defining structure is to be found. By selecting a cylindrical form, the new building has neither a front nor a rear façade, and fails to give any pronounced town planning signal. What is, however, significant is the fact that the auditorium's shape clearly emphasizes the central position and significance of the building within the campus. Its basic form lends the building a pronounced monumental dimension and gives it an expressive power that associates it with a significant, similar auditorium on the campus.

The point of departure is a closed box situated within a glass volume. This represents an interesting variant on a design for an auditorium in Gosselies (1988) which was never built. The fundamental concept is also repeated in the design for the Grand Auditorium (Aula Magna) at the Catholic University in Louvain-la-Neuve. Here, the principle of the double skin has been applied in a creative fashion, in spite of a very limited available budget. The building is a near-classical construction in three parts: there is a concrete plinth with small windows, a transparent façade in glass, and a simple roof that converges to form a single tip.

Although experts often cite the poor acoustic properties of the cylindrical form, this powerful geometric shape has nonetheless been strictly adhered to. In response to a fascination for the historical antecedent of the Greek theatre with its good acoustic properties, a circular plan has been chosen for the auditorium. An important prerequisite to obtain good acoustics is the steep slope, a feature which also enhances the auditorium's visual properties.

The seating can be reached via gangways on two sides and one central gangway that takes the form of an 'S'. This 'S'-form arose so that the best seats could be placed in the middle of the space as well as in response to the requirement to adhere to strict safety regulations. The auditorium has four entrances, two of them at the upper end. Fluorescent tube fixtures supply a quasi-uniform lighting level. Air is drawn in above the auditorium; used air is extracted beneath the seating. A heating and cooling system is only present in the actual auditorium.

The maintenance of a visual link with the exterior also formes part of the design. Daylight reaches the auditorium via narrow horizontal openings. The slope of the auditorium also determines the space in the foyer. The glass permits an unexpected view onto the campus. At night, the building looks like a giant lantern in the heart of the campus.

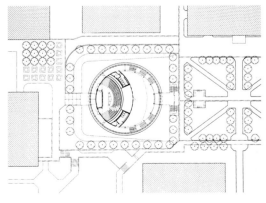

Site plan

Client:
Brussels Free University
1992-1993

The illuminated building

Exterior view with entrance

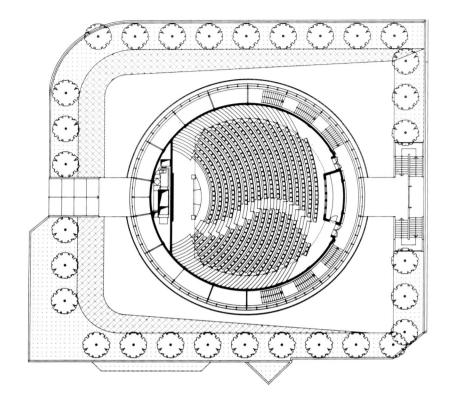

Plan of the auditorium

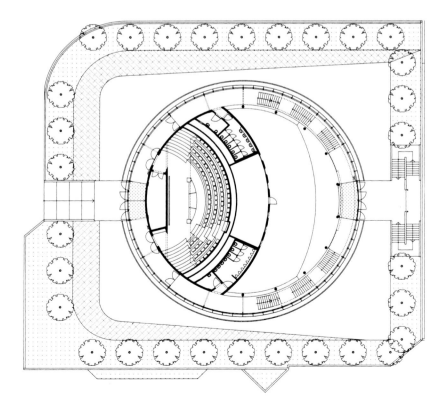

Plan of the entrance level

Interior view of auditorium

View of the foyer

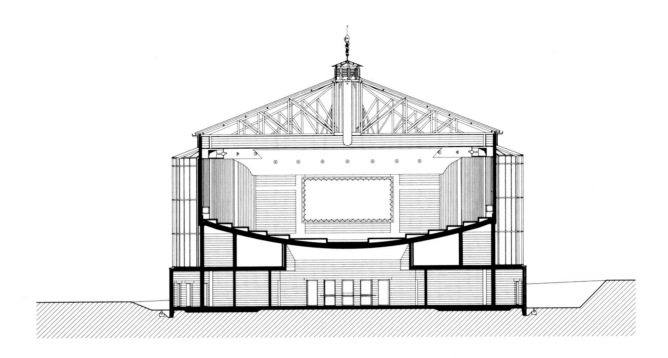

Cross-section

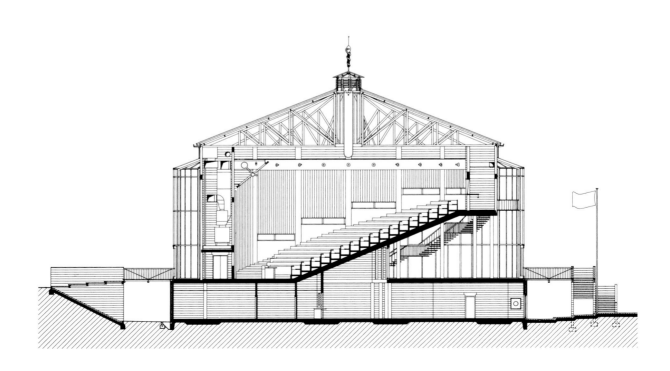

Longitudinal section

Interior view from the entrance of the foyer with staircase

Interior view to the entrance of the foyer with staircase

Back in 1935, the city of Brussels commissioned the building of a large complex at De Heizel in order to house the large international exhibition of that year. It was built from a design by the architect Joseph Van Neck. Since then, the complex has become the most important Belgian exhibition space for various commercial events. The most important Belgian trade fairs are held here. The 1958 World Exhibition was also integrated into the complex; the front façade was given added emphasis through the construction of the famous Atomium along the building's axis line.

The creation of a very large parking lot to the rear of the complex (for 12,000 cars), with a direct link to the motorway, resulted in most visitors entering by the rear entrance. The north side thus became the principal façade. This fact became increasingly problematical and demanded a drastic solution. Hence the owner organized a design competition, which was won by the Samyn architectural practice. Two particular elements made a major contribution to this favourable decision: a town planning approach, and the strong architectural form chosen for the new building's design.

The first part of the project has already been constructed – it forms a wooden bridging construction that links the large parking lot with the trade fair complex. The preliminary design opted for a gently sloping glass roof that was reminiscent of a huge sailcloth. The site is triangular in shape. The roof is slightly sloping across its widest zone. The roof surface becomes increasingly steep on approaching the most acute angle in the triangle. At its edge, the roof itself merges into the frontage – this is the position where an adjoining office building is due to be added. There will be a new entrance hall beneath the huge roof. This area will provide the space for all the necessary services. The project is primarily intended to allow the introduction of a new distribution pattern permitting easy access to all the various neighbouring halls. The design also involves the construction of a 600-metre internal street in a zone that is currently fully built over.

In a sweeping gesture, the triangular open space is being transformed by the presence of the new front façade. After the project design was completed in 1996-1997, the client decided against staggering the construction over successive phases (as originally foreseen), but without any major increase in the budget. This resulted in a fundamental rethink of the design. The elegant wooden rafters were replaced by a simplified wooden structure and the intended glass roof acquired a standing seam aluminium roof cover. This was executed in an inventive fashion, with the necessary attention being paid to the penetration of light into the interior. Given the cost of 18,000 BEF (446 Euro) per square metre, this represents a major achievement. In addition, it is now apparent that these incisive modifications have given the design a simpler and more imposing demeanour. The project is due to be completed in the year 2000.

Client:

Parc des Expositions de Bruxelles
1995-2000

Site model

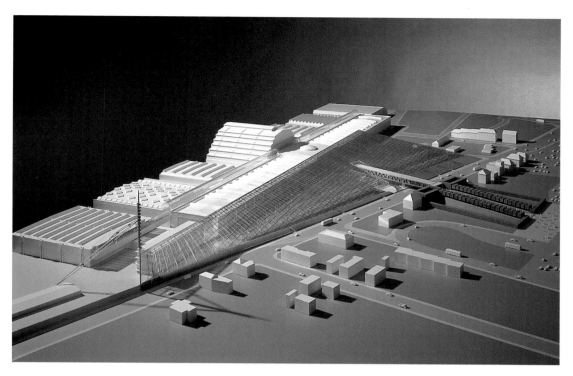

Model of the large roof unifying the north side of the exhibition centre

Computer image of the roof structure (design stage)

Structural model (design stage)

Pedestrian bridge from the car park to the exhibition centre

Temporary exterior access to the pedestrian bridge

Interior view of the pedestrian bridge

AULA MAGNA, UNIVERSITÉ CATHOLIQUE DE LOUVAIN | Louvain-la-Neuve, Belgium

Louvain-la-Neuve is the only new city to be created in Belgium in the 20th century. At the end of the 1960s, the ancient Catholic University of Louvain was split to form two distinct independent institutions. This saw the French-speaking section move to a new home in Louvain-la-Neuve, located between Brussels and Namur. The new town plan foresaw a radical split between motorized traffic and pedestrianized areas. The aim was to give it the appearance of a naturally green settlement which led to the abundant use of brick in its construction.

The town's central square had to wait many long years for an appropriate solution. This formed a very desolate urban space, with an open view onto a big lake on one side. The Samyn practice was awarded the commission to devise a master plan in which the new Grand Auditorium was to assume a central position. The town planning design foresaw a denser building volume and a site for the auditorium between the square and the water surface. The design agenda for the "Aula Magna" required that it be capable of accommodating 1200 people and offer an infrastructure that could support a wide variety of events and activities.

The idea behind the auditorium is that it should act as a large urban hall, a new alternative design along the lines of the basilica designed by Andrea Palladio for the Italian city of Vicenza. The core of the "Aula Magna" is its large auditorium which is surrounded by a glazed shell. The main concept behind the auditorium has already been used in other works: a compact building within a shell. This major project also offers a unique opportunity to apply the principle of the double shell with all its ensuing consequences. This is an energy-efficient concept that requires little addition of heat in the winter or mechanical air conditioning. Its layout contains a clear logic that is determined by the design agenda

as well as the site. The technical and constructional solutions have been carried out with the utmost precision so as to arrive at a balanced clarity. There is no need to explain the technology behind the solution; everything has simply been applied to attain maximum control.

The mere choice of materials used in the construction of this building represents a radical break with the artificial small-scale character of Louvain-la-Neuve. Following the example set by architect André Jacqmain's library of 1970, the "Aula Magna" has assumed the right to individuality that can be accorded to important public commissions.

The whole site is characterized by a special layout. The main entrance to the "Aula Magna" is on the town square side. Access to the foyer is via a low room located beneath the podium of the auditorium. This is a very imposing space that gradually increases in height; it contains a series of staircases as well as the passageways to the auditorium. The ceilings in the foyer and the auditorium both possess an identical slope. From the foyer, there is a wide view across the large lake. The lifts are located at the four corners of the building. The vertical rear wall of the auditorium is conceived as a large projection screen that can be seen from the town square. In order to allow scenery and large objects to be brought inside, a raising platform is provided at the entrance. The auditorium, in parallel with the entire volume, is of a strict and restrained composition. The sitting area is divided into three zones; the middle zone has continuous seating. Daylight is also allowed to penetrate into the auditorium.

In a recent development in the town plan, it has been decided to construct a cinema complex to the left of the auditorium with a connecting museum. This decisive evolution is designed to attach more weight to the town centre.

Client:
Université Catholique de Louvain
1996-2000

Site plan

Longitudinal façade with emergency staircase along the façade

Lateral façade at night

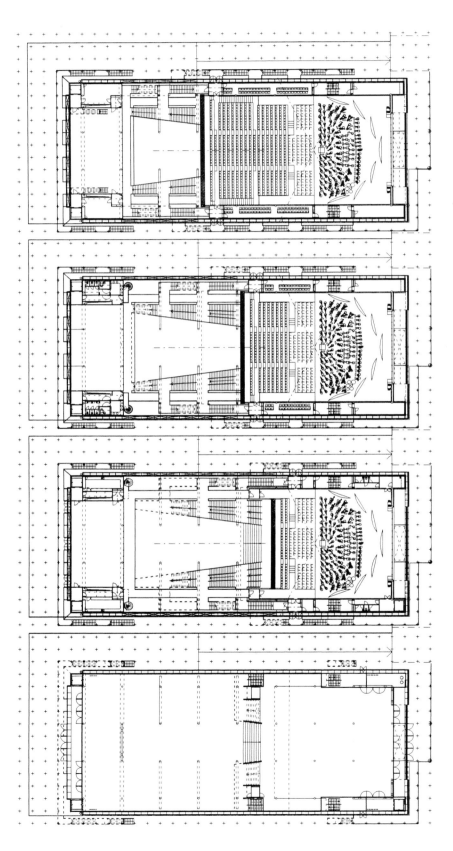

Plans (from bottom to top)

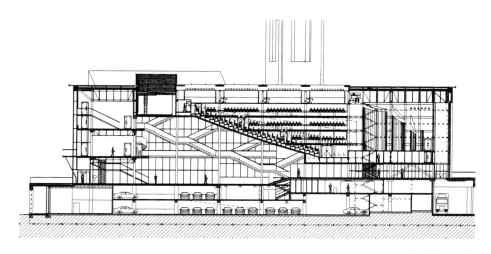

Longitudinal section

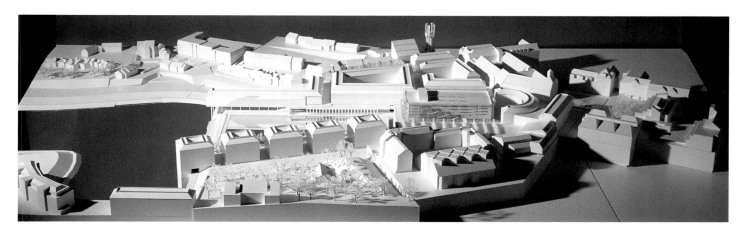

Model of the urban planning proposal

View to the stage

View from the stage

Entrance lobby

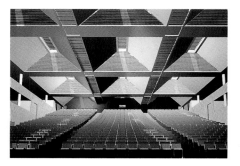

COLLABORATORS

On April 1st 1999, the team SAMYN AND PARTNERS is composed
of 55 collaborating architects, civil engineers, administrative and technical staff, of which:

10 ACTIVE PARTNERS
Philippe SAMYN, Architect, Civil Engineer, Principal Partner
Denis MELOTTE, Civil Engineer-Architect
Antonio QUIÑONES, General Secretary
Johan VAN ROMPAEY, Civil Engineer-Architect
Bernard VLEURICK, Architect
Fawas EL SAYED, Civil Engineer-Architect
Ghislain ANDRE, Architect
Yves AVOIRON, Architect
Jacques CEYSSENS, Architect
Michel VANDEPUT, Architect

3 NOMINATED
Quentin STEYAERT, Architect, Nest NEUCKERMANS, Civil Engineer-Architect, Frederic BERLEUR, Architect

6 EMPLOYEES (of which 3 for rooms and machinery upkeep)
In order of arrival since 1978:
J. GONZE, H. D'HUIS, P. HATTO, A. HENRI-JASPAR, N. van HAELEN, M. Ch. ARNOULD, B. DARMSTAEDTER,
F. BEYNS, J. NAIM, A. de BONGNIE, M. TYCKAERT, J. NAIM, M. HAEST , N. SEGUIN have successively been in charge of
the secretarial department, and at present kept by D. MAYALIAN.
Dr. Ing. J.-L. CAPRON, assisted by A. CHARON, A. VAN DER LINDEN et V. LECLERC, is in charge of the publication
department.

36 ARCHITECTS AND/OR CIVIL ENGINEERS
In order of arrival since 1978: Ph. SAMYN, M. VANDEPUT, G. DEVUYST, B. COLIN, R. DELAUNOIT, J.P. DE GRAEF,
P. HOUSIEAUX, N. LAPORTE, L. HENS, G. BRYS, D. VAN HOLE, C. DASSARGUES, J VERSCHUERE, M. VILLE,
A. CHARON, J. MOUVET, Ch. VAN DEUREN, D. SPANTOURIS, C. VEDOVATO, D. MELOTTE, L. FINET, J.L. DEBAR,
C. SCHEID, S. VANDROOGENBROECK, M. MOLLAERT, J. VAN ROMPAEY, B. NEY, P. WILLOCX, E. ROBERT, M . QUENON,
A. MASHAYEKH, F. JANSSEN de BISTHOVEN, W. GOOSSENS, A.F. de FROIDMONT, Y. AZIZOLLAHOFF, W. VERBRIGGHE,
T. HAC, E. COLLIGNON, E. WATHIEU, V. CARPENTIER, J. COSYN, W. AZOU, M. MIGEOTTE, B. VLEURICK, S. GAYDA,
T. KHAYATI, J. CEYSSENS, Ph. TIRCHER, Q. STEYAERT, Y. BUYLE, P. DUTHOIT, I. AKKAN, A. ANTOINE, B. SELFSLAGH,
A. CANTARELLI, D. MOREL, M.J. DITTGEN, M. BENKIRANE, M. NAJEM, M. BOUZAZAH, H. DOSSIN, A. MESTIRI,
P. KAPITA, M. VAN RHIJN, M. van RAEMDONCK, P. DE NEYER, R. MERTENS, M. RAMOS, K. DELAFONTEYNE,
J. HAENSENDONCK, D. SINGH, A. GOOD, P. MANDL, A. HEMAMOU, J.P. DEQUENNE, F. COURTOIS, M. FAIDHERBE,
M. BERCKMANS, D. VERBOVEN, Th. ANDERSEN, O. DEMOULIN, B. DEWANCKER, P. VERLEYEN, W. DORIGO,
T. BOLING, I. de CLERCK, M. RENCHON, F. EL SAYED, Th. SYDOR, W. VAN LAER, Ch. GODFROID, J.-L. CAPRON,
C. EMBISE, H. HEINEMANN, A. LAHLOU MIMI, B. LEGRAND, C. ZURECK, O. PESESSE, A. O'HARE, A. d'UDEKEM
D'ACOZ, I. MARTIN BENITO, N. MILO, N. VANDENDRIESSCHE, Th. BERLEMONT, T. de le VINGNE, V. VAN DIJCK,
F. LAMMENS, G..BLERVACQ, M. PATEL, S. OST, CH. FONTAINE, H. KIEVITS, Gh. ANDRE, T. CONTENT, R. TAPIA MICUCCI,
S. PEETERS, Y. AVOIRON, K. DE MULDER,T. PROVOOST, Th. HENRARD, D. PEREMANS, J. DAELS, O.VERHAEGEN,
P. GOETHAELS, J.Y. NAIMI, A. FRANCIS, F. KEUTGENS, N. BROMBRANT, L. KAISIN, A. BRODZKI, F. LERMUSIAUX,
R. PANSAERT, B. de MAN, M. ACHTEN, M. RUELLE, Ch. DE NYS, T. LEJEUNE, D. CULOT, J.L. RODRIGUEZ SAMPER,
C. VANHAEREN, S. VERHULST, G. VAN BREEDAM, J.-F. ROGER FRANCE, Á. ÁGÚSTSDÓTTIR, V. DERAMEE, F. BERLEUR,
Ph. VAN CAENEGHEM, N. NEUCKERMANS, F. QUENUM, J. de CALUWE E. KRZESLO, W. DHAENENS, I. DELATTRE,
L. GESTELS, M. di BARTOLOMEO, R. HOUBEN, S. SWIGGERS, F. LEONARD, G. VAN DER VAEREN, P. LATTEUR, R. KIM,
D. CARRION, G. DEHARENG, P. DE CARRELO, B. CALCAGNO, B. DARRAS, S. REITER, T. LOUWETTE, E. VAN MEERBEEK
have contributed for at least 6 months or are still contributing to the team's work.

Engineering studies are carried out with SAMYN and PARTNERS' two subsidiaries:
SETESCO (structural) with main Civil Engineers: Jacques SHIFFMANN, Guy CLANTIN, Philippe SAMYN, Luc SOTTIAUX
and FTI (services) with main Civil Engineers: Jean Michiels, Philippe SAMYN, Jeffrey DE CALUWE.

WORKS & PROJECTS

in Belgium when no country stated | * in association | (c) competition entry | (r) renovation

1972 Built works:
- DE BACKER residence*
- WING TABLE
  Projects:
- 60-storey high-rise WING building
  Theorical studies:
- ISOBARRES-ISONODES:
  structural morphology studies

1973 Built work:
- RICHIR residence
  Projects:
- LE GROGNON, Namur*
- DOUALA RAILWAY STATION, Cameroun*(c)
  Theoretical studies:
- BELGIAN PATENT on double curvature
  shells with corrugated steel sheets
- BRUSSELS POPULATION
  DENSITY LIMIT STUDIES
- HIGH-RISE BUILDINGS IN AN URBAN
  CONTEXT, VERTICAL AND SPATIAL
  CITIES

1974 Built work:
- NYSSENS residence
  Projects:
- VAN WEDDINGEN apartment building
- CYLINDER CUBE kinetic sculpture
- MAELBEEK VALLEY master plan*

1975 Built works:
- ROSE, SAMYN, MARTIN,
  and first BOGAERT residences
- POLICE STATION Brussels Royal Parc
- SAINT AUGUSTIN CONVENT Brussels
  (Structural engineering for Architect
  Ch. Van Deuren)
  Projects:
- VOKAER and VALENTIN residences
- NURSERY prototype buildings
  Theoretical studies:
- STRUCTURAL SYSTEMS FOR
  HIGH-RISE BUILDINGS,
  a theorical survey

1976 Built works:
- ORBAN*, DE RIDDER,
  first VAN GINDERDEUREN*,
  and BOULANGER* residences
- AEROCONDOR travel agency
- KOEKELBERG high school nursery*
- STRUCTURAL ENGINEERING
  of support and chimneys
  for offshore industrial boilers
  Projects:
- RENCHON, COLLARD, MEUWESE,
  MWAMI NDATABAYE NGWESHE
  WEZA III residences
- ROSE apartment building
- KOEKELBERG high school sports hall*

1977 Built works:
- second and third VAN GINDERDEUREN
  dwelling units, DEGOEYSE*, ROSIER*
  residences, and four SOGERIM houses*

- VAN DEN BERGH showroom (structural
  engineering for Architect Ch. Van Deuren)
  Projects:
- VAN DEN DRIESSCHE,
  DE FABRIBECKERS, DEHAEN,
  and JANSON residences
- WATERLOO high school master plan
  and sports centre
- VEEWEYDE animal nursery

1978 Built works
- 8 WERISTER houses, DUHOUX and
  second BOGAERT residences,
  two AMART houses
- FOYER LAEKENOIS 254
  social housing units (r)*
- CGER-ASLK 24 apartments
- LEUZE HIGHSCHOOL restaurant,
  sports hall and four classrooms
  Projects:
- 4 houses for S.A. CONSTRUCTION
- VAN GINDERDEUREN, 3 housing units
  and FRUY private residence

1979 Built works:
- FRANCO and TURIELS apartments,
  Nice, France
- PIRLOT, JOOSTENS,
  and LEPARLIER residences
- GIFT PROMOTION exhibition stand
- EUROP CENTER office building (r)
- UNION DES DRAPIERS shop
  Projects:
- DARMSTAEDER, WISSINGER, GONZE,
  SAMYN, and DEWITTE residences
- VAN GINDERDEUREN apartment building
- FOYER LAEKENOIS 44 new housing units
- PRION PANSIUS DOMAIN
  park development and 5 houses
- WYBUNIT participation in the
  development of Jacques Wybauw's
  system of building construction
- CENTRAL BANK OF BELGIUM
  office building (r) (c)

1980 Built works:
- CITY OF BRUSSELS 16 apartments
- MTARA MAECHA private residence,
  The Grand Comoro Island*
- SIMAK office building
- CENTRE MADOU office building (r)
- WATERLOO high school
  Projects:
- VAN CUTSEM 5 dwelling units
  and 8 apartments

1981 Built works:
- SAMYN, VAN HECKE,
  and PARDOU-LEYSEN residences
- SIMAK 12 apartments
- SAMYN AND PARTNERS offices,
  first extension
- ABEILLE-PAIX and STAR EUROPEAN
  PROPERTIES various office buildings
  new and (r)

- BEAUDET dental consulting rooms
- ATHUS secondary school
- COMMUNE D'ETTERBEEK 43 apartments
  and 9 shops: structural engineering
  sa COTE D'OR feasibility studies
  Project:
- ALEXANDRE residence

1982 Built works:
- NIVELLES secondary school
  for the handicapped
- BEULLENS and LOUVEAUX residences
- AG SECURITAS office building (r)
- TRAVAUX & METALLURGIE,
  stand Batibouw
- SAI LAMP, halogen lamp
  with articulated arm
- LEVI-STRAUSS and Co. Continental
  Europe Headquarters, interior design
  Projects:
- LAPORTE residence
- BWW prototypes of steel
  orthotropic floor slabs
- ENTREPRISES FERRET, inhabitable
  cylindrical hall featuring metal foundations
  and orthotropic floor slabs with a
  wrapping allowing for easy assembly and
  dismantling, requiring no external
  resources or sources of energy.
  Intended for desert areas
- LEVI-STRAUSS headquarters
- EUROPEAN BANK for LATIN AMERICA
  office building (r)
- KATHMANN-INTERNATIONAL,
  expertise of chicken farms, Lybia

1983 Built works:
- LEVI-STRAUSS BELGIUM, Trade Mart
- SB and PARTNERS
  offices and showroom (r)
- ROYALE BELGE office building
  Projects:
- ABEILLE-PAIX office building
- NOVOTEL 100 bed hotel
  Theoretical studies:
- FOLDAWAY INTERNATIONAL, studies
  for a folding and unfolding living unit
- REYNOLDS CONSUMER, studies of an
  aluminium and cast aluminium garden
  furniture line in kit form

1984 Built Works:
- FARR and DEUTEKOM residences
  and 4 SOGERIM houses
- COBEMABEL offices and showroom (r)
- ABEILLE-PAIX office building (r)
- IN WEAR 4 shops
- SAMYN AND PARTNERS
  second office extension
- ASSURANCE LIEGEOISE,
  technical and building survey
  Projects:
- BERNHEIM-OUTREMER industrial buildings
- MINISTRY OF PUBLIC WORKS
  energy renovation

- AG old warehouse Van den Borre (r)
- MODRZEWSKI offices and showroom (r)
- LEVI'S JEANS exhibition
- CIG administrative complex

1985 Built Works:
- BISQUERET-RAMMER residence
- MENDEZ TRANSLATIONS
  office buildings (r)
- RTS EUROP offices
- CITIBANK computer processing centre
- GARDY S.A. office building(r) (*)
- CIMENTS D'OBOURG landscaping
  and interior design
- DESIGN BOARD design studio
- BIOLUX office building (r)
- ZURICH-VITA office building (r)
- VILLEBREQUIN-EXSABER 3 shops,
  Saint-Tropez, France
  Projects:
- VAN DER MEERSH residence
- RENAULT INDUSTRIE car plant (r) (c)
- ABEILLE-PAIX offices and apartments
- ENSAAV-LA CAMBRE,
  architectural degree project
- FLT CONTRACTORS 54 housing units
- ARCO CHEMICALS office building (r)
  Theoretical studies:
- D.V. FLUOR, study of lighting devices
- MINISTRY OF PUBLIC WORKS, partici-
  pation in the drawing up of the energy
  register for the Belgian state properties

1986 Built works:
- FORIERS and SAMYN residences
- O.B.C.E. stands, Luxembourg
- SHELL RESEARCH CENTRE,
  chemical research centre
- MINISTRY OF PUBLIC WORKS,
  Mons Law court, diagnosis and energy
  renovation
- DUPUIS printing factory
  Projects:
- BRUCKER SPECTROSPIN office building
  and laboratories
- GB-INNO-BM renovation
  of the "Au Bon Marché" general store
- BELGIAN AIRPORT CONSULTANTS
  (BEAC), Luqua airport, Malta
- FAMIBANK office building

1987 Built works:
- ANTOINE residence (partial)
- COLEN stand Batibouw
- MINISTRY OF PUBLIC WORKS,
  energy renovation of various state
  properties
- URBAINE-UAP
  office and apartment building
- RIVENDELL PROPERTIES office building*
- RENOVATION MAINTENANCE
  office building and industrial hall
- THOMPSON AIRCRAFT
  TIRE CORPORATION office building
- GENERALE DE BANQUE office building (r)

Projects:
- RUE DE LA LOI landscaping
- O.B.C.E. stands,
  Luxembourg and Madrid-Spain
- DELHAIZE supermarket
- CIG office building
- BONNEWIJN STOCKBROKERS
  townhouse renovation
- L'ASSURANCE LIEGEOISE office building
- BANQUE BRUXELLES LAMBERT, "Marnix"
  headquarters (c)
- AG GROUP massing plan
  and office buildings
- SOLVAY central chemical research centre
- CITYMO office building, "City 2"

1988 Built Works:
- CARBONELLE and G. SAMYN residences
- OLIVETTI office building (r)
- CIMENTS D'OBOURG head office,
  interior design
- FINA RESEARCH-PETROFINA
  cable stayed bridge
  and research centre (c)
- BOULANGER office building
- SINT LUKAS ARCHIEF-GENERALE BANK
  exhibition
- BRUVERD office building
  and warehouse
- O.B.C.E. stand, Barcelona, Spain
- GEPATIM office building (r)
  Projects:
- HAFERKAMP, WEISS, FRERE,
  and FUNCK residences
- AEROPORTOS E NAVEGACAO AEREA
  (ANA), airport, Punta Delgada-Sao
  Miguel, Azores
- SIGMART, beach cubicle (c)
- MORGAN GUARANTY TRUST COMPANY
  of NEW YORK, Euro-Clear Operation
  Centre (c)
- CATERPILLAR auditorium
- Mc KINSEY, "Hôtel Copee"(r)
- CITY CENTRE-AG GROUP offices, housing
  and retail complex
- SHELL BELGIUM, office building (r)

1989 Built works:
- BLANCO and SIMONIS residences
- PATRIMSA 8 apartments
- DONNAY-JANSSENS renovation
  of 3 apartments
- DUPONT DE NEMOURS showroom
- GENERALE DE BANQUE office building (r)
- M & G RESEARCH LABORATORY
  research centre, Venafro, Italy
- SIDMAR-ARBED-ALZ OCAS
  research centre
- BRUSSIMMO office building
- AUTOMATIC SYSTEM
  lifting barriers for cars
- IMMOBILIERE LOUIS DE WAELE
  Triomphe I office building
- BRUSSELS UNIVERSITY animal facility
- TEROTECHNOLOGIE factory

Projects:
- UNION CHIMIQUE BELGE (UCB)
  office building
- GONTHIER garden centre
- ZURICH GROUP office building (r)
- EUROPEAN PAVILION, Seville, Spain (c)
- VIDEOSCOPE office building (r)
- EUREAL housing complex
- VITA-ZURICH GROUP office building (c)
- KREDIETBANK headquarters (c)
- SONELEC water tower and national
  monument, Nouakchott, Islamic Republic
  of Mauritania

1990 Built works:
- ABEILLE-PAIX (r)
  Projects:
- O.B.C.E. stand Telecom (c)
- REPUBLIC of FRANCE,
  "Espace Moselle" (r) (c)
- 4 B BROTHERS interior design
- WANSON site planning
  Theoretical studies:
- FRACTALS, fractals of regular polygons
  and their projections on curved surfaces
  of positive and negative Gaussian curva-
  ture, fractals of regular polyhedra

1991 Built works:
- PORTAL workshops
- PETROFINA guest-residence I (r)
- PATRIMSA renovation of 4 apartments
- NISSAN European technology centre
- CITIBANK 55 branch offices
- BERHEIM-OUTREMER "Crystal"
  office building
- PORTAL EUROPE interior design
- STASSART farm residence - new Samyn
  and Partners offices (r)
  Projects:
- ASTRA GROUP, commercial development,
  Djakarta, Indonesia
- INR-NIR INSTITUT NATIONAL DE
  RADIODIFFUSION - NATIONAAL
  INSTITUUT VOOR RADIODIFFUSIE (r)*
- VVV WESTVLAAMSE BERGEN museum
- FOURCROY-STORK,
  industrial real-estate development
- NARA CONVENTION HALL, Japan (c)
- BELGIAN ARMY, office building
  and warehouses
- REPUBLIC of FRANCE,
  "Espace Poitou Charentes" (r) (c)
- ADVANCED ELASTOMER SYSTEMS,
  research centre
  Theoretical study:
- HARMONIC STRUCTURES

1992 Built works:
- BRUSSELS UNIVERSITY auditorium
- BRUSSELS UNIVERSITY campus square
- PATRIMSA 2 apartments
- DHERTE residence
- EFTA-AELE Brussimmo
  building interior design

- SIEMENS E.G. interior design
- WALLONIA FORESTRY CENTRE
  research centre
  Projects:
- SIEMENS headquarters
  and urban master plan
- ALFA ROMEO exhibition area and offices
- TREMA GROUP
  mixed-use development
- ALL-RUIGH bridge (c)
- PRO-JET, millwork workshop
- BLOOMERS HOLE LECHLADE,
  pedestrian bridge (c)

1993 In progress:
- CLINIQUE PSYCHIATRIQUE SANS-SOUCI,
  hospital
- CREOF, apartments, shops
  and office building
- SPONDA OY, Martini Tower (r)*
  Built works:
- BACOB, banking branch and 4 apartments
- DUPUIS PUBLISHING headquarters
- PATRIMSA residence (r)
- VAN DE PUT residence (r)
- BRUSSELS LAWYERS' BAR
  ASSOCIATION, interior design
- THE SQUARE CIRCLE, sculpture
- GEMBLOUX AGRONOMIC FACULTY,
  auditorium
- MERCK SHARP & DOHME, interior design
- 'T HOOFD SEGHERS ENGINEERING,
  office building (r)
  Projects:
- LION farmhouse (r)
- ORDRE DES DOMINICAINS, church,
  convent, apartments
- NEANDERTHAL museum (c)
- OFFICE PUBLIC D'AMENAGEMENT ET DE
  CONSTRUCTION 80 residences,
  Amiens-France
- SMITHKLINE BEECHAM headquarters I (c)
- INTERCOMMUNALE DU BRABANT
  WALLON master plan and office buildings
- ARAUCO, bridge, Santiago, Chile
- ENTEL, headquarters, Santiago, Chile (c)

1994 In progress:
- BRUGMANN UNIVERSITY HOSPITAL (r) (c)
  Built works:
- PETROFINA, restaurant
- FINA EUROPE, Wanlin service stations
- FORIER and PATRIMSA residences (r)
- SMITHKLINE BEECHAM
  bio-pharmacological research centre (c)
- CNP-COMPAGNIE NATIONALE à
  PORTEFEUILLE headquarters
- BANQUE BRUXELLES LAMBERT,
  "Marnix 3" office building (r)
  Projects:
- BRUSSELS UNIVERSITY, student club
- IPEO, master plan and office buildings (c)
- SMITHKLINE BEECHAM, master planning
  and landscaping
- DE CLOEDT, master planning

1995 In progress:
- ERASMUS metro station
- CHATEAU DE SENEFFE "orangerie" (r)
- BRUSSELS EXHIBITION CENTRE
  visitor centre
  Built works:
- MULLIEZ residence (r)
- PATRIMSA, 3 apartments
- SWITEL Antwerp, hotel
- SMITHKLINE BEECHAM,
  landscaped parking lot
  Projects:
- UNION CHIMIQUE BELGE headquarters (c)
- FINA EUROPE, "Fina 2010" service stations
- LE CRACHET scientific
  and technical forum (c)
- DIERICK, VAN LOOVEREN & Co,
  office building

1996 In progress:
- AULA MAGNA, University of Louvain
- SMITHKLINE BEECHAM, oval car park
- FINA EUROPE, Uccle and Louvain-La-
  Neuve service stations
  Built works:
- CERTECH research centre
- JAPANESE AMBASSY,
  ambassador's residence, Luxembourg
- PETROFINA guest-residence II (r)
  Projects:
- LOUVAIN-LA-NEUVE western part
  of the city master plan
- ERASMUS HOSPITAL, landscaping (c)
- FINA EUROPE, service stations (r)
- TWO ALICE, hospital (r)
- SMITHKLINE BEECHAM BIOLOGICAL,
  headquarters II (c)
- BAGECI, office building (c)

1997 In progress:
- UNIVERSITY OF LIEGE, car park
- JEAN AND MARC DUMONT, office building
- CITY OF BRUSSELS, sports club
- PROCTER AND GAMBLE master planning,
  office building and visitor centre
- FINA EUROPE, Houten, service station
  Built works:
- ALBEMARLE, research centre
- PATRIMSA townhouse (r)
- SEGHERS manor (r)
- LEVI STRAUSS EUROPE interior design
- PATRIMSA offices and apartments
  Projects:
- CAISSE CONGE DU BATIMENT,
  office building (r) (c)
- SEGHERS ENGINEERING, master planning
- WILHEM & CO, 14 cinemas
- HALLEN KOOTRIJK, business center (c)
- INP-INSTITUTO DE NORMALIZACION
- PREVISIONAL, new headquarters,
  Santiago, Chile (c)

1998 In progress:
- FINA EUROPE, Orival highway,
  service stations and restaurant (c)

- THE SITE, office building
- CHATEAU DE MARIEMONT "orangerie" (r)
- INSTITUTE FOR CELLULAR PATHOLOGY,
  auditorium and library
- FIRE STATION, Houten, Netherlands
- UNIVERSITY of LOUVAIN, museum
- CODENS shelter
- TMB: warehouse and office building
- COMPAGNIE IMMOBILIERE
  DE WALLONIE, office building
- LCEBE, office building (r)
- SIBIX, office building (r)
- INR-NIR: concert halls and office building (r)*
  Projects:
- TOUR CENTRALE, office building (c)
- SMITHKLINE BEECHAM BIOLOGICAL,
  headquarters III (c)
- FINA EUROPE, Froyennes, service stations,
  restaurants and 80 bed hotel (c)
- CANAL PROPERTIES, office building
- FINA RESEARCH, access control building
- ENTE IDROCARBURI NAZIONALE (ENI),
  Rome-Italy (c)
  Theoretical study:
- INTERNALLY STAYED BRIDGE, proposal
  for a 45m span pedestrian bridge as a
  first application of the theoretical
  research on harmonic structures and
  internally stayed trusses + patent

1999 In progress:
- Bridge and riverbank landscape,
  Copiapó, Atacama Region, Chile
- KINEPOLIS cinema complex extension
  and world headquarters
- CEI Headquarters
- KINEPOLIS, Madrid, Internal refurbishment
- TOTAL FINA; Hellebecq, service stations

BIBLIOGRAPHY

- Emery Marc & Sowa Axel, "Comptoir forestier, Belgique", L'ARCHITECTURE D'AUJOURD'HUI n° 322, 1999/05, cover + p. 25 & pp. 90-97; (FR).
- van Bergeijk Herman & Mácel Otakar, GUIDA ALL'ARCHITETTURA DEL NOVECENTO BENELUX, Electa, Milano, 1998, pp. 37-78-82-89-92-93; (IT).
- Krewinkel Heinz W., GLASS BUILDINGS; MATERIAL, STRUCTURE AND DETAIL, Birkhäuser, Basel - Boston - Berlin, 1998, pp. 80-83; (CH).
- Samyn Philippe, "Structural morphology", TRANS ARCHITECTURES 02 + 03: Cyberspace and emergent theories, AEDES, Berlin 1998; (DE).
- Capron Jean-Luc, "Textile Membranbauwerke - eine ausgereifte Technologie: Projekte von Samyn & Partners", in: BAUEN MIT TEXTILIEN, 1998/11, Ernst & Sohn - Wiley, pp. 11-15; (DE).
- Samyn Philippe & Latteur Pierre, "Displacements of Structures, Applications to Classical and Harmonic Structures", Proceedings of the 1998 IASS SYMPOSIUM: Lightweight Structures in Architecture, Engineering and Construction (edited by R. Hough and R. Melchers), Sydney, 1998, pp. 362-367; (AU).
- Samyn Philippe, Latteur Pierre & van Vooren John, "Volume of Structure, Application to Classical and Harmonic Structures", Proceedings of the 1998 IASS SYMPOSIUM: Lightweight Structures in Architecture, Engineering and Construction (edited by R. Hough and R. Melchers), Sydney, 1998, pp. 537-545; (AU).
- Capron Jean-Luc, "Samyn and Partners: Contextual Use of Steel", JOURNAL OF CONSTRUCTIONAL STEEL RESEARCH Vol. 46, n° 1-3, 1998, pp. 123 & paper number 413 (full paper on CD-ROM), Proceedings of the SECOND WORLD CONFERENCE ON CONSTRUCTIONAL STEEL DESIGN, Elsevier, 1998; (GB).
- Roger-France Jean-François, "L'architecture 'verte' a-t-elle un avenir ?" - "Zit er toekomst in een 'groene' architectuur ?", A PLUS n° 152, 1998/06-07, pp. 51-54; (BE).
- van Bergeijk Herman & Mácel Otakar, BIRKHÄUSER ARCHITECTURAL GUIDE - BELGIUM - THE NETHERLANDS - LUXEMBOURG - BIRKHÄUSER ARCHITEKTUR FÜHRER BELGIEN, NIEDERLANDE, LUXEMBURG, Birkhäuser, Basel-Berlin-Boston, 1998, pp. 37, 78-79, 82, 89, 92-93; (CH).
- Jacobs Steven, "Kantoorgebouw Seghers Engineering", Jaarboek ARCHITECTUUR VLAANDEREN 1996-1997, Ministerie van de Vlaamse Gemeenschap, pp. 174-175; (BE).
- Melet Ed, "Transparent en toch energiezuinig", DE ARCHITECT, 1998/06, pp. 72-75; (NL).
- Samyn Philippe, Capron Jean-Luc & Roger-France Jean-François, "An Ecological and Economical Design Approach of Timber Buildings by Samyn and Partners", Proceedings of the 5TH WORLD CONFERENCE ON TIMBER ENGINEERING (WCTE) volume 2, Ecole Polytechnique Fédérale de Lausanne, 1998, pp. 416-423; (CH).
- Marquez Jaime R. & Tapia Rodrigo, "Construcciones para los cinco sentidos: entrevista a Philippe Samyn", C.A. - Revista Oficial del Colegio de Arquitectos de Chile A. G. n° 92, 1998/01-03, cover + pp. 78-83; (CL).
- Samyn Philippe, "Poutre en treillis et pont comportant une telle poutre - Lattice girder and bridge comprising such a girder", Demande de brevet Européen n° 98.87.01.009, 1998, 22 pp.; (EU).
- Samyn Philippe, Capron Jean-Luc & Roger-France Jean-François, "The double-skin facade: a sustainable solution for a better environment", FACADE EN KLIMAAT, Uitgave Faculteit Bouwkunde, TU-Delft, 1998, pp. 7-1 t/m pp. 7-16; (NL).
- Samyn Philippe, "Recent projects of Samyn and Partners", Proceedings of the INTERNATIONAL CONFERENCE ON ENGINEERING A NEW ARCHITECTURE, Aarhus School of Architecture, 1998, pp. 71-80; (DK).
- Samyn Ph., Wouters P., Martin S. & Roger-France J.-F., "The Aula-Magna: a 1200 seat multi-purpose hall for the Université Catholique de Louvain conceived to save maximum energy", Proceedings of the WORLD RENEWABLE ENERGY NETWORK INTERNATIONAL CONGRESS - V, Firenze, 1998, pp. 1341-1344; (IT).
- Samyn Ph., Wouters P., Martin S. & Roger-France J.-F., "CCB-VKB: Refurbishment of an existing office building designed to reduce its energy consumption below 100 kwh/m^3 per year", Proceedings of the PLEA'98 (Passive and low Energy Architecture) INTERNATIONAL CONFERENCE, James & James, 1998, pp. 299-302; (PT).
- KORTRIJK 1990 - 2000 - Projecten voor een stad, selectie; "BUSINESSCENTRUM DE HALLEN". Meervoudige opdracht, 1997, Facetten 3, centrum voor Architectuur en design (cAD), 2 pp; (BE).
- VLAANDEREN NIEUWE ARCHITECTUUR, Prisme, Brussels, 1997, pp. 130-131, 154-157, 205-206; (BE).
- Loze Pierre, "Réaffectation de deux constructions de la fin du XVIIIe en lieu de spectacles et de conférences" - "Herbestemming van twee gebouwen uit het einde van de 18de eeuw als theater - en conferentiezaal door Samyn en Partners", A PLUS n°147, 1997/08-09, pp. 58-61; (BE).
- LES CARNETS D'ARCHITECTURE CONTEMPORAINE n° 2 Philippe Samyn: maquettes, CFC-Editions, Bruxelles, 1997, 96 pp.; (BE).
- della Fontana Jacopo, SAMYN AND PARTNERS: ARCHITECTURE TO BE LIVED, l'Arca, Milano, 1997, 171 pp.; (IT).
- Schock Hans-Joachim, SOFT SHELLS, Design and Technology of Tensile Architecture, Birkhäuser, Basel - Berlin - Boston, 1997, cover + pp. 26-30, 43-47 & 136-140; (CH).
- "Walloon Branch of Reproduction Forestry Material", SPACE DESIGN n° 389, Tokyo, 1997/02, pp. 36-37; (JP).
- SCHWERPUNKT HOLZ IN MURAU, 1996, pp. 10-13, 38-53, 154-155, 165-168; (AT).
- WALLONIE NOUVELLES ARCHITECTURES, Prisme, Bruxelles, 1996, pp. 134-135, 166-167, 172-173, 180-181, 184-185, 208-209, 215-216; (BE).
- Samyn Philippe & Steyaert Quentin, "La structure chez Horta, particulièrement l'Hôpital Brugmann", MEMOIRES DE LA CLASSE DES BEAUX ARTS (Actes du colloque Horta), Académie Royale de Belgique, 3ème série, tome XII, Mémoire n°1979; 1997, pp. 31-56; (BE).
- Aron Jacques, Burniat Patrick & Puttemans Pierre, L'ARCHITECTURE CONTEMPORAINE EN BELGIQUE, GUIDE - DE HEDENDAAGSE ARCHITECTUUR IN BELGIE, GIDS - CONTEMPORARY ARCHITECTURE IN BELGIUM, A GUIDE, Les Editions de l'Octogone, Bruxelles, 1996, pp. 66, 72, 75, 76, 78, 86, 92, 101, 113, 123, 178, 181, 188, 226; (BE).

- De Meulder Bruno, "De Heizel, kruispunt van tijd en ruimte", ARCHIS, 1996/08, pp. 67-80; (NL).
- Samyn Philippe & Capron Jean-Luc, "Double Skin Buildings as a Step Towards Sustainable Architecture", Proceedings of the PLEA (Passive and Low Energy Architecture) 13TH INTERNATIONAL CONFERENCE, Université Catholique de Louvain, Louvain-La-Neuve, 1996, pp. 437-442; (BE).
- Samyn Philippe & Capron Jean-Luc, "Temperate Intermediate Spaces and Virtual Thickness of Inhabited Façades", Proceedings of the PLEA (Passive and Low Energy Architecture) 13TH INTERNATIONAL CONFERENCE, Université Catholique de Louvain, Louvain-La-Neuve, 1996, pp. 431-436; (BE).
- Loze Pierre, "Démarche: Samyn et associés" - "Ontwerp Samyn & partners", A PLUS n° 139, 1996/04-05, cover + pp. 32-45, 54 & 77-79; (BE). See also an erratum in A PLUS n° 140, 1996/06-07; (BE).
- Samyn Philippe, "La petite ville possible de trente mille habitants", BULLETIN DE LA CLASSE DES BEAUX-ARTS, Académie Royale de Belgique, 6ème série, tome VII, 1996, 1-6, pp. 131-137; (BE).
- Robbin Tony, ENGINEERING A NEW ARCHITECTURE, Yale University Press, New Haven - London, 1996, pp. 20-23, 102, 132 & fig.17; (US).
- "Showing the Seeds", THE ARCHITECTURAL REVIEW n° 1189, 1996/03, pp. 3, 33, 68-71; (GB).
- Daniels Klaus, "Laborgebäude M. & G. Ricerche, Venafro", in: TECHNOLOGIE DES ÖKOLOGISCHEN BAUENS, Birkhäuser, Basel - Boston - Berlin, 1995, pp. 276-277; (CH).
- Melet Ed, "Le Comptoir Wallon van Philippe Samyn", DE ARCHITECT, 1996/02, pp. 74-77; (NL).
- Machado Rodolfo & el-Khoury Rodophe, MONOLITHIC ARCHITECTURE, Prestel Edition, München-New-York, 1995, pp. 18, 19, 51, 75, 76, 136-147, 170, 172; (US).
- Samyn Philippe, "Walloon Branch of Forestry Reproduction Material", Proceedings of the ASIA-PACIFIC CONFERENCE ON SHELL AND SPATIAL STRUCTURES, CCES-IASS APCS, Beijing - China, 1996, pp. 138-145; (CN).
- Samyn Philippe & Kaisin Laurent, "Harmonic Structures: The Case of an Isostatic Truss Beam", Proceedings of the ASIA-PACIFIC CONFERENCE ON SHELL AND SPATIAL STRUCTURES, CCES-IASS APCS, Beijing - China, 1996, pp. 255-262; (CN).
- BRUXELLES: VILLE NOUVELLE - HET NIEUWE BRUSSEL - BRUSSELS NEW CITY, Prisme, 1995, cover + pp. 42-48, 100-101, 132-133, 140-143 & 241-242; (BE).
- Bekaert Geert, ARCHITECTURE CONTEMPORAINE EN BELGIQUE, Editions Racine - HEDENDAAGSE ARCHITEC-TUUR IN BELGIE & CONTEMPORARY ARCHITECTURE IN BELGIUM, Editions Lannoo, 1995, pp. 190-191, 206; (BE). See also: A PLUS n°140, 1996/06-07, p. 16; (BE).
- Dubois Marc, "Ökologisches High-Tech", ARCHITEKTUR AKTUELL n° 185, 1995/11, pp. 52-59; (AT).
- Samyn Philippe, Mélotte Denis, Clantin Guy & Mollaert Marijke, "Tanken in een tent", BOUWEN MET STAAL n° 128, 1996/01-02, pp. 22-26; (NL).
- Dubois Marc, "Ecologische high tech. Le Comptoir Wallon van Philippe Samyn", ARCHIS, 1995/10, pp. 35-39; (NL).
- Toepfer W., "Constructec-Preis 1994 - Europäischer Preis für Industriearchitektur", DBZ Deutsche Bauzeitschrift, 1995/02, pp. 105-110; (DE).
- "Kantoorgebouw Brussimmo, Brussel", BOUWEN MET STAAL n° 123, 1995/03-04, cover + pp. 36-39; (NL).
- Márquez Jaime, "Pasarela peatonal de Ph. Samyn en Santiago", C.A. - Revista Oficial del Colegio de Arquitectos de Chile A. G. n° 77, 1994/07-09, p. 19; (CL).
- Samyn Philippe, "Auditorium, Vrije Universiteit Brussel. Open naar buiten, gesloten naar binnen", BOUWEN MET STAAL n° 118, 1994/05-06, pp. 47-49; (NL).
- Schulitz H.C., "Research Centre for the M. and G. Ricerche Chemical Company", INDUSTRIEARCHITEKTUR IN EUROPA, CONSTRUCTEC PREIS 94, Ernst & Sohn, Berlin, 1994, cover + pp. 35-36 & 42-51; (DE).
- JAARBOEK ARCHITECTUUR VLAANDEREN 1990-1993, Ministerie van de Vlaamse Gemeenschap, pp. 16, 94-97; (BE).
- Samyn Philippe, "Principios de construcción", C.A. - Revista Oficial del Colegio de Arquitectos de Chile A. G. n° 76, 1994/04-06, cover + pp. 48-53 & 61-64; (CL).
- "Wooden Shell for Belgian Forestry Department", PROGRESSIVE ARCHITECTURE, 1994/08, p. 20; (US).
- Melet Ed, "Streven naar het optimale", DE ARCHITECT, 1994/03, pp. 80-87; (NL).
- QUATERNARIO AWARD (International Award for Innovative Technology in Architecture, Singapore 1993), Electa, Milano, 1993, pp. 98-101; (IT).
- "Bürohaus Rue Bélliard", BAUWELT n° 40/41, 1993/10/29, pp. 2196-2197; (DE).
- Sartori Alberto H., "Philippe Samyn", C.A. - Revista Oficial del Colegio de Arquitectos de Chile A. G. n° 73, 1993/07-09, pp. 136-137; (CL).
- Aron Jacques, Burniat Patrick & Puttemans Pierre, LE GUIDE DE L'ARCHITECTURE MODERNE A BRUXELLES, Les Editions de l'Octogone, 1993, cover + pp. 331, 422-425 & 480-482; (BE).
- "Form and Structure: recent works of Samyn and Partners, Architects and Engineers", SPACE DESIGN n° 346, Tokyo, 1993/07, pp. 69-96; (JP).
- Capron Jean-Luc, " 'WHY ?': An interview with Philippe Samyn", SPACE DESIGN n° 346, Tokyo, 1993/07, pp. 89-91; (JP).
- Dubois Marc, BELGIO. Architettura, gli ultimi vent'anni. Tendenze dell' architettura contemporanea, Electa, Milano, 1993, pp. 30, 41, 158-161; (IT).
- Verboomen Stephane, "Office building in Waterloo", SPACE DESIGN n° 344, 1993/05, pp. 65-73; (JP).
- "Zelt mit komplizierter Innenwelt", ARCHITEKTUR AKTUELL n° 157, 1993/04, pp. 32-35; (AT).
- Capasso Aldo, Majowiecki Massimo & Pinto Vincenzo, LE TENSOSTRUTTURE A MEMBRANA PER L'ARCHITET-TURA, Maggioli Editore, 1993, pp. 24, 53, 124, 127-129; (IT).

- "Stählerne Archetypen", ARCHITEKTUR AKTUELL n° 156, 1993/03, pp. 44-47; (AT).
- Fisher Thomas, "Steel Research Center", PROGRESSIVE ARCHITECTURE, 1992/02, p. 101; (US).
- "Travail en douceur", TECHNIQUES ET ARCHITECTURE n° 404, 1992/10-11, pp. 57-59; (FR).
- Samyn Philippe, "Tuibrug Petrofina, Feluy", BOUWEN MET STAAL n° 107, 1992/07-08, pp. 42-46; (NL).
- E. V., "Building Chemistry", THE ARCHITECTURAL REVIEW n° 1143, 1992/05, pp. 67-70; (GB).
- Dubois Marc, S/AM, Stichting Architectuurmuseum 92(02), 1992/04-05-06, pp. 22-34; (BE).
- Loze Pierre, "Démarche: Philippe Samyn et associés" - "Demarche: Samyn en Vennoten", A PLUS n° 115, 1992/03-04, cover + pp. 42-52; (BE).
- Samyn Philippe, "Laboratorium M. en G. RICERCHE, Venafro (I)", BOUWEN MET STAAL n° 105, 1992/03-04, pp. 19-24; (NL).
- Samyn Philippe, Schiffmann Jacques & Ruelle Michel, "Poutres et treillis tridimensionnels en mailles triangulaires à progression harmonique", IASS Proceedings of the FIRST INTERNATIONAL SEMINAR ON STRUCTURAL MORPHO-LOGY, Montpellier, 1992, pp. 441-453; (FR).
- Loze Pierre, "Immeuble de bureaux à Waterloo. Entretien avec Philippe Samyn" - "Kantoorgebouw te Waterloo. Gesprek met Philippe Samyn", A PLUS n°114, 1992/01-02, pp. 40-43; (BE).
- Samyn Philippe, "Steel and Textile Structure: Appropriated Technologies", Proceedings of the IASS (International Association for Shell and Spatial Structure) International Symposium, Copenhagen - Denmark, "SPATIAL STRUCTURE AT THE TURN OF THE MILLENIUM" Volume II: Structural Form, Kunstakademiets Forlag Arkitektskolen, 1991, pp. 187-194; (DK).
- BUILDING DESIGN n° 1017, 1991/01/11, pp. 1, 22-27; (GB).
- Arcidi Philip, "Beyond Technical Finesse", PROGRESSIVE ARCHITECTURE, 1990/12, pp. 76-77; (US).
- Aron Jacques, Burniat Patrick & Puttemans Pierre, GUIDE DE L'ARCHITECTURE MODERNE - BRUXELLES ET ENVIRONS 1890 - 1990. Itinéraires - Didier Hatier, 1990, pp. 124-127; (BE).
- "Young Architects Issue", PROGRESSIVE ARCHITECTURE, 1990/07, pp. 76-77; (US).
- Damen H., "Aanbouw als meubel: uitbreiding Design Board in Ukkel", DE ARCHITECT n° 21/3, 1990/03, pp. 41-45; (NL).
- PROFIL D'UN ARCHITECTE - PROFIEL VAN EEN ARCHITEKT, Sint-Lukas Archief, 1989, 112 pp.; (BE).
- Samyn Philippe, "Chemical Research Centre Shell Louvain-la-Neuve", A PLUS n° 101, 1988/04, pp. 33-35; (BE).
- Samyn Philippe, "Lieux de travail et technologie" - "Werkruimtes en technologie", A PLUS n° 101, 1988/04, pp. 26-32; (BE).
- "Vorschule in Aubange", DETAIL Zeitschrift für Architektur + Baudetail, 1987(3), pp. 266-270; (DE).
- Peirs Giovanni, LA TERRE CUITE, L'ARCHITECTURE EN TERRE CUITE APRES 1945, Mardaga, 1982, p. 170; (BE).
- TECHNIQUES ET ARCHITECTURE n° 338, 1981/10, pp. 142-143; (FR).
- "Des maisons dans la pente. Maisons individuelles à Rhode-Saint-Genèse, Belgique", TECHNIQUES ET ARCHITEC-TURE n° 338, 1981/10, pp. 144-145; (FR).
- DETAIL Zeitschrift für Architektur + Baudetail, 1981(1), pp. 26-28; (DE).
- Samyn Philippe, "Voiles minces à surface doublement réglée", NEUF n° 57, 1975/09-10, pp. 26-27; (BE).
- Samyn Philippe, "Structures isobarres et isonoeuds", Proceedings of the 2ND INTERNATIONAL CONFERENCE ON SPACE STRUCTURES, University of Surrey, Guildford, 1975, pp. 621-634; (GB).

- L'ARCA
  n°135, 1999/03; n° 134, 1999/02; n° 126, 1998/05; n° 124, 1998/03; n° 123, 1998/02; n°117, 1997/07-08; n°116, 1997/06; n° 110 1996/12; n°107, 1996/09; n° 102, 1996/03; n° 101, 1996/02; n° 100, 1996/01; n° 98, 1995/11; n° 90 , 1995/02; n° 88, 1994/12; n° 87, 1994/11; n° 80, 1994/03; n° 79, 1994/02; n° 76, 1993/10; n° 75, 1993/10; n° 72, 1993/06; n° 70, 1993/04; n° 69, 1993/03; n° 65, 1992/11; n° 57, 1992/02; n° 55, 1991/12; n° 54, 1991/11; n° 49, 1991/05; n° 48, 1991/04; n° 45, 1991/01; n° 42, 1990/10; n° 41, 1990/09; n° 39, 1990/06; n° 37, 1990/04; n° 32, 1989/11; n° 31, 1989/10; n° 30, 1989/09; n° 24, 1989/02.

- L'ARCA INTERNATIONAL
  n° 26, 1999/01; n° 22, 1998/05; n° 21, 1998/03; n° 18, 1997/11; n°15, 1997/07-08; n°14, 1997/06; n°8, 1996/12.

- L'ARCA PLUS
  n° 17, 1998.

ILLUSTRATION CREDITS

(reading from left to right and from top to bottom, im. = image)

© I.T.P. : p.8 - im.1
© Guido COOLENS nv : p.74 - im.1
© HANNAERT-SCRIPT : p.10 - im.1
© Serge BRISON : p.76 - im.1
© Studio CLAERHOUT : p.16 - im.2
© Matteo PIAZZA : p.6 - im.1; p.63 - im.1; p.65 - im.1-2; p.66 - im.1; p.67 - im.1-2-3
© DAYLIGHT LIEGE sprl : p.69 - im.1
© Jan VERLINDE : p.51 - im.1-2; p.53 - im.1-2-4; p.55 - im.1
© F. LOZE & ARCHIPRES Paris : p.37 - im.1; p.38 - im.1; p.41 - im.2-3-4; p.81 - im.1; p.84 - im.1; p.85 - im.2
© André CHARON : p.22 - im.1; p.56 - im.1-2; p.102 - im.1; p.103 - im.2
© Andres FERNANDEZ : p.13 - im.3; p.20 - im.1-2; p.22 - im.4; p.53 - im.3; p.113 - im.1; p.119 - im.2
© Philippe SAMYN : p.70 - im.1
© Jean-Michel BYL : p.34 - im.1
© J. BAUTERS : p.9 - im.1-2-3-4; p.12 - im.1-3; p.13 - im.1-2; p.15 - im.1-3; p.16 - im.1; p.17 - im.1;
    p.18 - im.3; p.19 - im.1; p.22 - im.3; p.26 - im.1; p.30 - im.1; p.64 - im.1; p.112 - im.1; p. 114 - im.1
© Ch. BASTIN & J. EVRARD : cover; p.11 - im.1-2-3; p.15 - im.4; p.16 - im.3-4; p.17 - im.2; p.18 - im.4;
    p.25 - im.1-2; p.27 - im.1; p.29 - im.1-2; p.31 - im.1; p.35 - im.1-2; p.38 - im.2-3; p.41 - im.1;
    p.43 - im.1-2; p.44 - im.2; p.46 - im.1; p.48 - im.1-3; p.49 - im.1; p.69 -i m.2; p.71 - im.1;
    p.73 - im.1-3-4; p.75 - im.1-2; p.77 - im.2; p.79 - im.1-2; p.82 - im.1; p.85 - im.1-3; p.95 - im.1;
    p.96 - im.1; p.97 - im.1; p.107 - im.1-2; p.109 - im.1-2; p.111 - im.1-2; p.114 - im.2; p.115 - im.1-3;
© Marc DETIFFE : p.44 - im.1; p.47 - im.1; p.48 - im.2; p.49 - im.2
© SAMYN and PARTNERS : p.18 - im.1-2; p.54 - im.1; p. 70 - im.1; p.73 - im.2; p.77 - im.1; p.81 - im.2

© SAMYN and PARTNERS : all the drawings and computer images